INSPIRED LIVING

TEN STORIES OF TRANSFORMATION AND TRIUMPH

JENNIFER SPARKS   CAROLYN S. SCHRADER

AMANDA KORTHUIS   DIMPLE MUKHERJEE

BEAUTY H. FAULKNER   LERAE S. FAULKNER

SHERRI M. SWIDROVICH   ROBIN HILTON

LOIS A. UNGER   JENN KERR GASPAR

NICOLENE WATSON

INSPIRED LIVING, Volume 1
Copyright © 2019
STOKE Publishing

ISBN: 978-1-988675-53-4
LARGE PRINT EDITION

All rights reserved. No part of this book may be reproduced, scanned, or distributed in any printed or electronic form without permission from the individual authors/publisher. The opinions expressed within are those of each author and do not replace the consultation of a medical doctor, professional psychologist, or counselor if you have medical or mental health concerns.

Some names and places within these chapters have been changed or omitted to protect the privacy of the people involved.

Author photo credits are listed in each chapter.
Edited by Hilary Elmgren

If you would like to use the book in a group setting, please contact hello@jennifersparks.ca for bulk purchases at a discounted price.

Contact information for individual authors can be located in their chapter.

CONTENTS

Introduction	v
1. She Whispers	1
2. Seven Families, No Home: Surviving the "Sixties Scoop"	25
3. Written in the Stars	49
4. From Grief to Gratitude	69
5. Unshakable Love	89
6. From the Woman in Me to the Woman in You	117
7. Dying in My Presence	135
8. Layers of Love	155
9. It's All In Your Mind	179
10. Losing My Grip	197
Afterword	221
About The INSPIRED LIVING and INSPIRED BUSINESS Book Series	225
Please Leave A Review	229

INTRODUCTION

WISDOM AND GRACE

By Jennifer Sparks

This project has been percolating within me for some time. I needed the right authors to make volume one what I had imagined it would be.

I wanted stories that made people think. I wanted stories that made people feel. I wanted stories that would have readers waiting eagerly to find out more. I wanted stories to *inspire living despite circumstance or personal history*. When I found them, INSPIRED LIVING was born.

The format of each chapter is the same; the author summarizes their story (if you want the full story, many have or will have their own solo books) and then there is a question and answer section based on their experience.

What was most important to me was asking questions that would encourage the author to share with us the wisdom they now carried within and the grace that allowed them to come out the other side and feel inspired by and/or wiser because of their experience And then it came to me that wisdom from life experience, when shared, is grace multiplied.

I knew that my questions would encourage each author to think about their story from a different perspective too and some even commented that they learned things about themselves in the process.

These questions were designed to encourage the authors to share the deepest and most profound pieces of knowledge with you so that you get an immediate takeaway that can help you uplevel your life. We all face challenges at one point or another, and each chapter offers takeaways that can help you navigate life and all it throws at you - both the blessings and the obstacles. Each has a purpose, and together they create our lives.

While each of the stories is different, there are common threads about life, love, loss, transformation, and triumph that run through them.

As luck would have it, I know each of these women and have come to know their stories. As a publisher, I wanted to create a project that would allow their stories to be shared across networks, tables, coffee, amongst friends and across the world. Each of them lives an inspired life in some capacity despite what they had to walk through, and this is where I wanted the focus to be. I wanted the readers to be inspired to feel hope, strength, resiliency, and love. These women have faced adversity and come through to the other side with wisdom to share. This is their gift to the world. Please accept it freely.

What is your story?

Take the time to remember and honor your story. It's sacred. The wisdom contained in it may set you and others free.

1

SHE WHISPERS

AMANDA KORTHUIS

"From pain comes possibility."

AMANDA'S STORY

And there I was. Standing in the middle of a gravel pit thinking this was the end. I felt trapped. With me in the car was my husband, and my boys, ages one and three. Nothing made sense. How had I, a strong, stubborn, spiritual woman with big dreams, ended up here? I was barefoot, nearly naked and alone in the woods, trying to escape alive.

You see, for years I never saw a way out, I never saw any hope for a different future, and I truly believed that if I left, he would hunt me down and kill me. He had told me that in fact. I had no reason to doubt him. Therefore, with that belief seared into my mind, coupled with the belief that marriage was forever, I stayed and built a life within the prison walls of his mental illness.

His snore startled me from my thoughts and brought me back to reality. I looked all around me. How could I get us out of here alive? Where could we run? How could I run with two kids in tow? I slowly started to unlock the car doors to try and get my two babies out of the back seat, thinking that maybe if I ran fast enough, I could make it to the edge of the forest before he woke up.

"What are you doing? Get back in the car," he barked. I instantly panicked and shut the door.

"I was trying to take the boys outside, so they didn't wake you, and you could rest. Owen needs to pee. I have to change the baby's diaper." After a few grumbles and muffled words, he fell back asleep.

My heart was racing. I opened the door and quietly got my kids out. I told my three-year-old to stay beside mommy. I held my baby in my arms and slowly walked around to the trunk of the car. There I was standing in my bare feet in a gravel pit, the dark, thick forest looming over me, the sun setting. I hoped someone would find me before it was too late, but as the daylight started slipping behind the mountains, my hope dwindled.

I quietly opened the trunk, hoping to find diapers for the baby. As my eyes adjusted to the light, what I saw took my breath away, and reinforced my deepest fears. Today I was going to die, leaving my boys to suffer at the hands of their drug-addicted and mentally ill father.

And as I stood in the forest, looking up to the sky, the rain started gently washing my tears away. I whispered to myself; *I won't do this anymore. I can't do this anymore.* I knew that if I stayed surely, I would die, but if I escaped, I might have a chance to survive.

That moment in the forest was the end of my life as I knew it. The next 24 hours was the start of losing everything I knew about myself. I stood in the forest in a tube top, and jersey shorts, no shoes on my feet, no wallet to prove my identity - completely and utterly alone. But at that moment, I knew that I had to survive. Death was not an option. I had survived eleven years with this man; I could survive four more hours of driving back to safety.

With that, I gathered my babies, and got back in the car and did what I had spent eleven years doing. I realized then that I had become an expert in survival. This insane cycle of abuse had become so routine I did not realize how far removed from the world I was. I leaned over, gently laid my hand on his chest, and whispered in his ear, "I'm sorry. I'm sorry for all the pain I've caused you. I'm sorry for being unfaithful. I'm sorry for hurting you. I'm sorry I failed as a wife to make you happy." Even though not a word of that was true, I went on to say, "Please forgive me, and pray for me so that my sins will be forgiven."

Then he woke up, and he looked at me and said, "It's not up to you to decide if you need forgiveness. It's up to me to choose *if* I will give it to you. If you're good enough, and you behave, maybe I will forgive you."

That day we made it home, but that day is just the beginning of my story.

Even though this horrific trauma, I still did not

believe that I was a victim of domestic violence. In fact, I judged women who claimed they were victims of domestic abuse thinking that their faith must not be strong enough to get them through it. I was spiritually conditioned to believe that my husband's happiness was my sole responsibility and that for me to experience freedom, I had to forgive him for all his wrongdoings and turn the other cheek. Even as I packed my bags to go into hiding at a transition house for battered women and children, I still didn't believe it. I would tell myself, my life wasn't that bad, and I wasn't that kind of women. I would try to justify my reasoning reminding myself that he didn't hit me every day, I never had a broken bone, and besides, he loved me. He was my other half, my spiritual guide, my lover, the father of my children, and my best friend. Not my abuser. I made excuses for him to hide my shame, and try to make sense of the chaos. I looked for reasons to explain why I had ended up here.

How did this church-going, deeply spiritual girl with big dreams end up nearly naked in a forest with two babies in her arms and her life on the line? I spent the next few years trying to answer that question. It was not until I held a book in my hands called *When Love Hurts* that I started to recognize myself in the stories. I saw that there is so much more to abuse than physical. As I read, I saw how every one of the twelve categories of abuse had permeated my life. The abuse was so ingrained in who I was that I didn't even know it was happening to me.

My therapist helped me see that it was not my spiritual duty to forgive the unforgivable. She went on to explain that I did not **let** any of it happen. She explained the manipulation, what abuse was, and she helped me see the damage of spiritual narcissism. She told me I was a victim of the worst kind of brainwashing she had ever seen.

It was with this knowledge that I went on to rebuild my life. I refused to carry his sins any longer within my body and mind and spirit. I fought fervently to heal. I discovered running as a means to self-nurture and through this shed nearly 100 pounds. I lived by the mantra that there was no time to be bitter and that there was work to be done. I lived each day with gratitude, thankful to be alive.

People always ask how I could survive all of that and not be bitter? The truth is, that night in the forest I saw what my life had become, and I knew that I was not who I wanted to be. I was finally free to choose for myself for the very first time, and I would not waste one precious minute being bitter, or staying stuck in the hell that I had known. I felt like I could finally breathe for the first time.

I had pulled insidious threads of abuse from my brain and knew that forward was the only way back to myself.

FIRESIDE CHAT

I first met Amanda on Instagram because one of her posts caught my eye and on occasion, I would connect privately with her. One day, she posted a short paragraph about being in the woods with her children and talked about how important it was to share these stories to protect others who may find themselves needing help to get out and stay away. Her story has many layers to it, so I am anxious to learn more about what she feels is most important to share.

People go through negative experiences, but eventually, some people can look at that experience and pull some things from it that they are grateful for, even though the experience has been difficult. Are you able to pull things from your experience that you are grateful for and if so, what are they?

I did not think I would survive that day in the forest, and when I did, there was no way for me to know what my life would look like after escaping. Every day I was stepping into the unknown, faced with choices I had to make that would completely change the outcome. I had to learn to make choices without the reassurance from anyone else that it was the right choice. It was incredibly scary, and I don't think words can capture and articulate the depth of pain and loneliness a person goes through when they are trying to flee a dangerous situation. As humbling as it was to go from being a wife, mother, and homeowner, to a single mom on social assistance, I am deeply grateful for the grace that was brought to my life. A period of time devoted entirely to learning, healing and developing skills to cope with life after abuse. I'm grateful for learning that the choice to leave was made in survival mode; the decision to not go back was made with my higher brain.

I spent eleven years in survival mode, and although I understood the definition of the term, I did not understand what it was doing to my brain. Our brains have three parts, and being in survival mode makes our body produce too much cortisol, which can be damaging. When we are functioning in this way, our body is responding to each situation in such a state of stress and high alert, and we cannot think reasonably or act rationally. To be able to use the reasoning part of our brain, the body needs to be in a safe, and relaxed state. Being in an abusive relationship, I went through cycles of being on high alert, and then going back down to honeymoon, relaxed state, and then back to walking on eggshells and then back to being on high alert again. Simply put, my brain was fried. I am so profoundly grateful for having this understanding because it helped answer the question of why I stayed. I stayed because it was all I knew. I only lived from one episode to another, and I was unable to see beyond that. I was trapped in a cycle of abuse. And so to say I am grateful for nearly dying in a forest sounds crazy, but it was that moment where I lost all fear of what might happen to me if I tried to leave. Because it was in the act of trying to survive that I saved my own life.

What has been the key success factors to coming through your experiences successfully, what wisdom would you share with others who may be facing the same type of challenge?

I was an overweight, exhausted and emotionally void mother of two young boys. Knowing that their future was 100 percent in my hands put a fire in my belly to become their rock and build a foundation of health, healing, and safety for them. Realizing I could not care for them unless I dealt with my demons, and faced my lifelong need to feel nurtured, was a critical moment of change. I learned how to self-nurture through the discovery of running. I learned what a calorie was and made myself accountable for everything that I ate. I learned how not to eat my feelings, and I went to therapy. I wrote in a journal, took parenting and fitness classes and I devoted my entire being to healing. I refused to be a bitter victim. I went on to lose 100 pounds, run a 10k race, and then a half marathon. My boys were my biggest fans and were at the finish line of every race I ran. Together we learned how to be physically and mentally healthy.

Someone once said to me that there was gold in the past and I did not know what that meant. It wasn't until I started facing my feelings, and allowed myself to grieve over the loss of what I thought my life was supposed to be, that I could fully embrace where and who I was. I came to terms with the reality that I was a victim of abuse, but that did not define me. I was not my abuse. I was not my trauma. It is a fine line between living in the past and learning from the past. I spent time going through my past, did a lot of learning and re-learning, and discovered that I had not been adequately nurtured. This ended up being a huge part of why I was stuck in the abuse. I believe that learning how to self-nurture through running gave me the strength to face all of the other challenges.

What would you do differently if you were to find yourself experiencing this even again as your much wiser self?

I don't know if there was anything I could have done to stop this from happening to me, but I do recognize that there was a moment that I stopped listening to myself. I suddenly started making choices that were not normal of my character. I was late for work, and I made excuses for not showing up to family events. I found myself ignoring my internal voice. The one that said, *Amanda, there is something not right here. This isn't like you.* Despite every red flag around me, my husband was fulfilling my need to be nurtured, to be accepted and loved by others. He fixed my insecurity and eased every heartache, so I never learned how to do it for myself. I look back and wonder if I would have known that my existence, my worth, and my place in the world was not dependent on a man, but rather that I was enough, and I did not need a 'soul-mate' to complete me, whether I may have been able to hear that internal voice and respond. If I had known that, I probably would not have rushed into marriage over the guilt and shame my religious upbringing taught me about sex outside of marriage. The belief that there is only 'one' soul mate, guilt over our natural physical desires and the feeling of never being good enough was a deadly combination that primed me for being the perfect target of this spiritual narcissist who knew how to meet every need, and draw me in faster than I could understand myself.

What role has letting go, surrendering, forgiveness, fear or limiting belief systems played in how much you suffered/succeeded?

Letting go, surrendering, forgiveness, fear and limiting beliefs can all act as a double-edged sword. In the faith that I grew up in, a common teaching is that forgiveness sets you free, that it is essential to let go, and put your troubles behind you, turn the other cheek, and be the bigger person. The guilt that comes from not being able to forgive is what kept me trapped in my marriage for as long as it did. I believed that to experience the peace that comes from God and the freedom that came from 'turning the other cheek', that I had to forgive the unforgivable. I spent eleven years begging for my husband's forgiveness. He insisted that I love him unconditionally, and forgive him for hurting me. He told me that I should pray for God to open my eyes and help me see what I was doing to cause him to behave this way and that maybe God and he would forgive me. Spending a considerable portion of my life repenting for sins I did not commit gave me a twisted understanding of forgiveness. It came to the point when even my facial expression, a muffled word, or hand on my head would trigger his rage and prompt me to beg his forgiveness.

Once I was away from the abuse, I began working on undoing the years of spiritual manipulation. I learned to separate my faith from what happened to me, and from all those rules and the idea that forgiveness meant pretending it never happened. I learned that forgiveness and acceptance are different things. Forgiveness does not mean tolerance. I learned that I could have a forgiving heart, without accepting how he treated me. For me, forgiveness was not pretending it did not happen, but rather, it was freeing myself from bitterness. I had anger, sure, but I was too busy getting better and did not have time for any of it. I was too busy working on discovering who I was, healing, and learning how to show up in the world, and what kind of mom I wanted to be. My old beliefs about forgiveness kept me trapped for eleven years, but this new understanding of forgiveness set me free.

What was the pivot point in the experience where things began to change for you in

terms of how you thought and felt about your situation? How did your thoughts and feelings change and how did that change impact the outcome?

For me, the pivot point came within the first couple of months of leaving. I was forced to seek help, which I would not have done otherwise. I went to a transition house, and through that, I was referred to a therapist. Amidst all of this, I had to go to court to get restraining order to protect my kids, and me, so he couldn't come after us. I was now in the court, social service, and therapy systems, and I felt so out of place because I did not see myself as a victim. I had too much pride to admit it, but when I let that all go and I learned to accept the help is when my heart opened, and I learned so much. I let go of my judgment of other people who I thought I couldn't relate to because I didn't see myself like them, and I also let go of judging myself. It was then that things started to change. I learned to embrace my vulnerability and accepting help. I realized that I was no different from anyone else, and it made me sit and wonder how many more women are out there like me. Women who don't see themselves as victims, because they go to church, have good jobs, whose husband is a youth pastor, who don't look like they are falling apart, but in reality are hiding deep secrets. When I let go of that judgment, it completely changed, me because I realized that I had so much to learn and that we are all the same. I learned how to be humble, that there was no shame in going on social assistance or accessing programs for moms who have been through abuse. I learned to accept help with how to parent, set boundaries, and I gratefully received food from the food bank, and a Christmas basket. All of these things forced me to swallow my pride, and that was probably the biggest thing that changed my outcome.

How has intuition served you on your journey? We often discount the intelligence that our "gut feeling" has - how has it served you?

The day I came home from shopping for my wedding dress my soon to be mother in law told me that it was my job to ensure my husband's happiness. If he wanted to go to school, move across the country, or spend his life in pursuit of accomplishing his own goals, even at the cost of my needs and desires, that's what I would need to do. The message was this is what it meant to be a loving, devoted and Godly wife. And so I lived by that fiercely, even though it meant death to the girl with big dreams. After years of abuse, torment and gut-wrenching pain, the voice inside of me was so quiet I could barely hear her. His voice echoed in my mind with every thought I had, and I would hear him telling me I'm crazy, I'm stupid, or I don't know what I'm talking about. I would have moments of clarity and think to myself that this wasn't what marriage was supposed to be, this wasn't 'of God', and then his voice or his mother's voice would roar in my mind, swirling me into such a state of confusion I didn't trust my thoughts. Shortly before leaving, a friend of mine said, "Amanda you've given eleven years of your life to this man. How many more are you going to give? You are a shell of the women you once were." I spent years thinking I was weak, and I needed him to 'help' me, teach me, and lead me. I believed that his happiness was my sole responsibility, and if I kept him happy to avoid conflict, I would keep my children and myself safe.

It wasn't one moment or one day, but a series of events and an accumulation of time that helped me to see, and open my mind. I started to undo the crazy, and begun to grab hold of my inner strength, and listen to that tiny little voice inside me. I could still hear her whispering, *your voice matters*. And when the time came, I trusted her. I trusted that I would survive that moment in the forest, trusted that I would survive the aftermath, and trusted that I would survive the recovery.

What are the top three lessons you have learned from this experience and how do they impact how you live now?

You're either strong, or you're weak

I had a very close relationship with a relative of my husband. This woman was tough as nails, having survived tragedy that great books are made of. I always said if I could be half the woman she was, I would be satisfied with who I had become. However, she was fiercely devoted to my husband, she loved him so dearly, like a son, so when I left my most profound regret was that I might lose my relationship with her as well. After we learned of my husband's death, she proved once again that her wisdom ran deep, and her love for me was beyond the loyalty of blood. She shared with me that she often wondered how I was able to get through this hell, how was I able to take this tragedy and flourish from the ashes, where my husband could not? Why was it that I took the pain and turned it into my fire, and he succumbed to his demons? She said, "Amanda, you are either strong, or you are weak. You are strong. He was weak." Sometimes we spend so much time wondering how we ended up somewhere, and we spend so much thinking about our pain that we end up paralyzed by our thoughts. The biggest thing my abuse taught me was that I have a choice. I can choose to give in to the pain that comes from trying to survive, or I can use all that strength to claw my way out to freedom, to live a life that is wild, brave and free!

Life isn't fair

This is probably one of my most common sayings with my boys to this day. Life is not fair. When we stop expecting life to be fair, we let go of expectation, and we can find strength and healing. Too often, we end up comparing our pain to someone else's, and that can keep us in a prison of bitterness. When we accept that the things that have happened to us, no matter how unfair, do not define us, we have the strength to rise above the abuse. When we embrace being a survivor, we can use the very pain that kept us a prisoner as a tool to push us forward. Life is not fair. But that does not matter. What matters is that you accept where you are, and move forward to where you want to be. When you put the focus on yourself, what you can do, how you respond, and what your choices are, you can walk through the unfairness with dignity and strength.

The peanut butter is yours

After escaping that day in the forest, my world completely changed. I found myself at the mercy of whatever help I could get. For me, I was so fortunate my parents had a trailer on their property my boys and I could make a home. The first night in the trailer, after I tucked the boys into their makeshift beds on the floor, I went to the kitchen to put away a box of food from the food bank I had received earlier that day. At that time, my pride was still considerable. I had always supported myself, paid my bills and took pride in being financially responsible. But in that last year before leaving my husband, not being able to work, and him draining our life savings on books, booze, and prescriptions, we found ourselves the recipient of the food bank more than once. If you have ever been on the receiving end of the food bank, you will understand when I say that peanut butter is the prized the item! In the few times we accessed the food bank before leaving my husband, I would be so happy to see peanut butter, as I knew my boys would love it. I would put it all away and wake up in the morning excited to make the boys toast. It never failed. Every time, I would open up the cupboard to find the jar empty. Scraped clean. As my husband's addictions escalated, so did his appetite, and he would eat uncontrollably at night leaving the boys and me nothing.

That night, in my new home, with the boys asleep I put away the items from the food bank, including the jar of peanut butter. I cried myself to sleep in my makeshift bed on the floor, and woke up stiffly in the morning to 'mama I'm hungry'. We went to the kitchen, not remembering what I had put away the night before, and opened the cupboard. To my shock, I saw the jar of peanut butter. Full. Untouched. I stood there and cried because I realized I was so conditioned to hoard food, that I expected it all to be gone.

At that moment I realized I would never have to

share my peanut butter ever again. The jar of peanut butter taught me that amidst losing everything I had ever known, that I was also gaining insights, I never expected. When you get so used to silencing your needs, your desires and your dreams, you forget that you have a voice. The peanut butter was mine, and no one could take it away from me. From that day forward everything that came through my doors, through my mind, and out of my mind was all my choice. I learned that it was essential to create a life that no one could take away from me. For me, this eventually led me down the path of building my own business, creating self-sufficiency and self-reliance.

Through my business, I learned a skill that no one can take away from me. I will never have to find an empty peanut butter jar or empty bank account ever again. By learning this, I discovered that I could let go of the fear of never having enough, or being enough. I am enough.

MEET AMANDA

Amanda Korthuis is a coach, author, inspirational speaker and the CEO of The Knotty Blonde, a lifestyle platform for women who are at the end of their rope. Her work focuses on teaching self-love and self-reliance as a means to overcome the deepest of fears so that her clients can create lives that are wild, brave and free.

Personal photograph

As Amanda was moving through her domestic abuse trauma, she quickly learned the importance of "creating knots" in her rope to keep herself from slipping into the abyss. With mounting pressures as a single mother, sole provider, caregiver and dealing with trauma fallout, Amanda learned how placing knots could propel her forward through tough times and help her deal with overwhelm and burnout.

Amanda is currently working on her solo book about her experience with domestic violence and spiritual narcissism. To learn more about Amanda's services and programs, please visit http://theknottyblonde.me

Backcover Photo Credit: Monika Broz

2

SEVEN FAMILIES, NO HOME: SURVIVING THE "SIXTIES SCOOP"

SHERRI M. SWIDROVICH

"These experiences helped to teach me that even if there are other people who hold power over me during the course of my life, I always hold the power to change those circumstances."

SHERRI'S STORY

As one of the 20,000 Indigenous children who were removed from their homes and families during a period known as the "Sixties Scoop," I spent a significant portion of my childhood in seven foster homes. The myriad of experiences I had while in care include various forms of abuse, leaving unforgettable legacies of pain, hurt and trauma. Those experiences are from my past, and do not make up the primary narrative of my current life. While I am proud to have survived this time, I am not fond of that title, since my experiences are in the past. Reflecting on what I have been through, however, makes me realize that my traumatic past is the catalyst that has allowed me to recognize and create the greatest joys and blessings of my life.

My entry into the foster care system was at the age of four. I have often referred to this placement as the "home from hell." The harsh treatment began when my sibling and I arrived at the home late in the evening. Almost immediately, in a small tin tub, we were scrubbed roughly, with a firm bristled brush. My new foster mother angrily berated us for being "such dirty little Indian kids."

The level of physical abuse quickly escalated, and we were punished in horrendous ways for the slightest of infractions. Among the most severe was being whipped with an electric frying pan cord. In a fit of rage after I had asked an overnight babysitter for breakfast, my foster mother ordered me to remove all my clothes and then return to the kitchen, where she began whipping me with the cord as I screamed out in pain and tried to shrink away from her striking distance. The next day, as the scabby wounds became visible, she expressed feigned shock and surprise, and attempted to absolve herself of all responsibility by claiming she couldn't have possibly caused every mark. It seemed to make her feel better when she applied the ointment to my skin. I just sat wordlessly, watching her, knowing we both knew the truth.

Beyond the physical, I experienced other forms of abuse there were equally traumatic and degrading. One evening at the supper table, I picked up a piece of chicken with my fingers to eat it. My foster mother backhanded me so hard that I fell off my chair. She commanded me to take the piece of chicken outside so I could eat it like the other animals, including biting into the bone and swallowing it. She then instructed her own boys to come and throw dirt on my food, saying animals also have to eat their food off the ground.

On the day I was rescued from the "home from

hell", I could not believe my luck and literally jumped for joy in the backseat of the car as I watched the house disappear in the dust of the long driveway. Unfortunately, my experiences in foster care were only about to get worse.

At the age of twelve, an indelible mark was made on my life when I experienced the trauma of sexual abuse from my foster father. Upon reporting the abuse to the authorities, I was called a liar, who was deemed to be like other *promiscuous Indian chicks, who liked to go out and have a good time and then cry wolf*. Despite taking, and passing a lie detector test, my foster father received minimal consequence for his actions. He had six months of probation, and few years later, was completely discharged. Because I reported him, I received the label of a *problem* foster child, and even future visits with my other siblings were closely supervised.

Enduring both physical and sexual abuse was traumatic, but the greatest source of anguish that still resonates with me today was having to accept the loss of the love and support of my biological parents and siblings. My whole world turned upside down when, at four years old, I was taken from my family. While we did have a few years together, by the time I was eleven, I was a permanent ward in the system, and became quite experienced at fitting in to other families and being able to refer to the parents as 'mom' and 'dad'. Even though I had a couple of wonderful foster parents, whose warmth, and care made a positive impact on me, I was still acutely aware that I was a stranger in somebody else's family. Feelings of isolation and residual sadness about losing the connection to my mom, and other family members remained, and I felt like an outsider for whom there was always something missing.

The pain of losing connection with my family helped fuel my desire to re-establish it. At a young age, I made a vow that I was going to be a mom and that I would make sure my children would never know what it was like to experience a childhood like mine. The desire to be a mother was such an intense dream for me, that it trumped anything else I could ever think of for my future. I realize even then that the yearning to create a family of my own was a manifestation of what I had lost as a child.

Thankfully, I met a man whose family values closely aligned with mine. I basked in the joys of raising our family and stayed focused on creating a happy childhood for them. Everything I had lost in childhood stood in such stark contrast to what I gained as a mom. I relished in each stage of growth with my children, and I never wished for a particular stage to pass by quickly.

The most positive outcome of my greatest childhood pain was that I received a new vision; an intense desire, and hyper-awareness of being able to give my family the complete opposite of my own experience.

FIRESIDE CHAT

I am not sure where to start with my questions as I am still focused on Sherri's ability to manifest a beautiful life from this place from which she came. I imagine her as a child in need of love and protection and wish I could swoop in and provide that for her, but I am amazed at how she uses these experiences to create a beautiful life.

People go through some negative experi-

ences but eventually some people are able to look at that experience and pull some things from it that they are grateful for, even though the experience has been difficult. Are you able to pull things from your experience that you are grateful for and if so, what are they?

It is easy for me to identify a specific example of something I am grateful for; in spite of the more negative context within which it took place, I still have so much gratitude for what happened in the aftermath. I would not have the special memories otherwise.

Despite the difficulties I experienced and the disconnect I had with my birth mother, I am overwhelmingly grateful for her, and how she showed up for me during the most difficult time in my life. Even though my mom no longer had any legal parental authority, she acted on a strong sense of intuition and showed up to help. I had just spent three days alone with my foster dad in a cabin at the lake, where he informed me, I was being groomed as a sexual partner. The last night had been the worst and I had laid there for hours dreading what was to come. The shock and joy of being woken up in the middle of the night to the sound of my mom's voice in the other room was overwhelming.

She had borrowed some money to take the train to the town where I was living, and she had no money to return home. The next morning, along with my mom, I walked out of my fifth foster home for the last time and together, we hitchhiked in mid-winter conditions to our hometown, a couple of hours away.

Although things were about to get worse for me again after reporting my foster father to the authorities, one of my greatest childhood desires was coming true. Even though I had had some intermittent time at home between placements, a great deal of anguish came from the heartache of the separation I had from my mom (and the rest of my family) during my years in foster care. Yet here I was, feeling safe and reconnected to her.

What happened next was the equivalent of a month-long sleepover with my own mother, and I finally experienced what it was like to have her undivided attention. She came to the police station with me, and she accompanied me when I took the lie-detector test. My parents were also separated but my dad would also come to visit, and I was ecstatic about this as well. Apart from the difficult circumstances that had brought us together, we had this time to grow close, and for me to see her enduring love, and the joy that she also felt in having me there.

On the very last day together, we rode the bus to the next major center, each on our way to separate destinations. As I got off the bus at my stop to wait for a social worker to pick me up and drive me to my next foster home, I looked up at her through the window. As part of an unspoken pact, we simply smiled and waved goodbye to each other. My heart was in a million pieces and one of the hardest things I have ever done was to fight the uncontrollable sobs that came over me as my mom drove off out of sight.

I am so grateful for this time with her. It strengthened my understanding that my mother loved me. This understanding gave me peace at various points in my life because I never doubted that I mattered greatly to her no matter what.

What are the key factors resulting in getting you to a place where you now possess

wisdom that you share with others who may be facing the same type of challenge?

The first thing that comes to mind in terms of what has brought me to the place I am now is being able to have my own family. As I shared in my story, the fact that I could have my very own family to love was in itself my joyful new beginning, and it simply drowned out any sense of loss or self-pity I may have continued to feel otherwise.

The second factor that has brought me to where I am now is that early on in life, I developed the ability to conquer my fears. Before I was taken into care the first time, my home was a one-room granary. The children ranged in age from about three to eleven years old; I was four. Except for the baby in the hammock, we were all lined up sideways on the bed. I remember one night the door latch had lifted due to the stormy conditions outside and the door itself was swinging back and forth, banging repeatedly in the wind. There was no electricity, and the night was cold and pitch black with scary noises coming from outside. Neither of my older brothers would get up and close the door, and I too, was scared to death of what or who could possibly be out there. Nevertheless, I threw off the covers and marched over, grabbed the door and hooked it in place. From an early age, I developed an ability to face and conquer my fears – no matter how big, or how small.

Much later, when my two oldest children were in school, I had contemplated going to University. I knew I was capable of putting in the effort to succeed, but I greatly feared failure. It was so overwhelming that I would have dreams about the professors somehow speaking an unrecognizable language, with me being the only one who could not understand what they were saying. The more I thought about wanting to do it, the more I knew I had to simply get up and go secure that door, again.

My intuition was also telling me to overcome my fears. One day there was a country music video on TV about a mom who goes back to school and despite some of the challenges with having a young family, she feels so much pride in her achievement. Seeing the video and hearing the song inspired me greatly. I wanted that too, and it fit with my desire to be at home still as much as possible.

Overcoming my intense fear of failure at University not only allowed me to gain a valuable education, but it also gave me the knowledge in order to reconcile my past with my newfound understanding about the colonial experience in Canada. I had carried a lot of shame about who I was, and these ideas were often a reflection of what I noticed in the world around me. However, through my University education, I gained important insight into the history of Canadian-Indigenous relations and the history of child welfare practices. I have gained a sense of pride and understanding about my Anishinabe background and my family and cultural history, and it thrills me to be able to teach and speak about these issues today.

What was the worst advice people gave you or the most annoying things that people said to you at difficult points in your journey? Explain.

One of the worst pieces of advice came from a social worker right after I ran away from my sixth foster home. My social worker felt there should be some accountability taken for my decision. In his mind, there was nothing wrong with my foster home, and so his conclusion was that if I chose not to return to my foster home, the only alternative was that I go to a juvenile delinquent home instead. Without assessing the impact on my mental and emotional well-being, my social worker focused only on the physical surroundings of the foster home, which to him, were satisfactory. I felt powerless in the situation, and felt as if he was being belligerent and bullying me. Additionally, his recommendation for the youth centre was terrible. While there, I experienced sexual advances from some of the boys during common activities and outings, and was offered illicit drugs, something I had zero experience with.

Moreover, it was also during my stay here when one of the most annoying things ever said to me by a professional was that "Sherri just needs a good cry." I had confided in my assigned social worker about many things I was having difficulty dealing with, in particular, everything that had happened after my disclosure of sexual abuse. I shared with her how much I continued to feel like an outsider and was known by many as the *foster kid* or the *Indian kid*. I shared how I thought this was what made me the subject of whispered taunts or gossip in my former small-town school. Most of all, and something I had expressed to my former foster mother was that I still had family members living in the foster home where I was sexually abused. The fact that they were still there told me just how invalid my experience and pain was to literally everyone in a position of authority. I also struggled with a sense of shame because no one took me seriously, despite taking a lie detector test to prove everything I said to be true.

After confiding these things to my social worker, and then seeing the recommendation written in my chart for a "good cry," it only further invalidated my feelings and concerns.

Within a few days, I began to carefully assess my surroundings and the level of supervision around our activities, as I evaluated possible opportunities to run. However, someone must have soon recognized the ill-advised placement and that I did not require being there, because without any explanation to me, I was pulled from the institution in less than two weeks.

What was the "pivot point" in this experience where things began to change for you in terms of how you thought and felt about

your situation? How did your thoughts and feelings change and how did that change impact the outcome?

One of the pivot points for me was when I finally got old enough to be able to exert some control over my own life, and I made the decision to run away from foster care. At the time, I was living in my sixth foster home, and had just become a teenager. That in and of itself, fed my anger and determination to do things *my way*. I was tired of being an outsider and isolated from my family. The only way I could see myself having unfettered contact with my family, while also gaining a greater measure of control over my own life, was to run away from my foster home, and to try to live life on my own. I laid these plans right after my arrival, but they incubated for quite some time before I was able to execute them. While I had no particular escape plan mapped out, the unwavering drive to leave provided the first step in allowing me to feel a greater sense of control over the circumstances of my life and gave me a greater sense of optimism about the future.

The outcome was that I ended up in the city where I would eventually create a home and a life for myself. Moreover, after a short stint in a youth detention centre, I also got the chance to live with my older sister for about three months. At this important time of my young adult life, the opportunity to reconnect and reminisce with her helped to begin the process of soothing many wounds. I have the warmest of memories about just how glorious it felt to spend this time with a family member of my own.

I know that the idea of running away probably does not make sense without the context, but for me, making and carrying out a plan that I made myself became one of the critical pivot points between my old and new life.

What are the top three lessons you have learned from this experience and how do they impact how you live now?

I did not immediately recognize that one of the most important lessons I took away from this experience was learning the significance (and the rewards) of being present in day-to-day living.

As a grandmother now, I often hear parents speak with regret about having been so busy or having wished their child to hurry and get through one stage of their life to the next. Certainly, we had busyness too, and were not literally always there, but the ability to be present is something I am blessed to have accidentally learned as a young mom. Today, I am even more keenly aware of just how much it is a pivotal aspect to living a life of fulfillment.

The second lesson I wish to include is what this taught me about the importance of overcoming fear in our lives.

The nature of my experiences created an array of challenges, a few of which I have shared here. While I don't hold the patent on this knowledge, I have gained some insight into how the fear of both real and imagined consequences can paralyze our decisions or prevent us from taking risks that carry the potential for life-changing outcomes. In being able to look back on what I have learned, I strongly believe that facing fears, making difficult decisions or dealing with a specific challenge in life is infinitely more rewarding and less painful than the outcome or the regret of not facing them!

The third lesson I have taken from all this is that even in seemingly powerless situations, we still have the ability to exert power and control over our own lives.

I was just six years old when I moved from the first extremely abusive foster home to a new placement. As an adult, I had the chance to visit this family again, and one of the things they remembered was how, upon our arrival, I had immediately warned them about not hurting my younger sibling. I have no memory of this, but they expressed surprise about how forward I was in my warning. Personally, I believe it may have also helped establish some parameters in the way they did treat us, because they clearly seemed to have realized I would never be quiet about such an issue.

There were many other untenable situations I had to face as a kid, over which I had little control. The lack of power forced me to find a way to act within the strict confines of my situation in order to bring about change in my life. On a couple of different occasions, that meant becoming a run-away, which was not necessarily an easy choice, but certainly a necessary one.

These experiences helped to teach me that even if there are other people who hold power over me during the course of my life, I always hold the power to change those circumstances.

How has intuition served you on your journey? We often discount the intelligence that our " gut feeling" has - how has it served you?

The role of intuition on my journey is compelling. However, the most extraordinary example stems from my mother's intuition, and not my own.

This experience happened when I was in a foster home where my foster father had an inappropriate sexual relationship with me. When he arranged an out of town trip together, on the pretense of 'winterizing' their cabin at a small lake, I felt nothing short of terror. Each night, he progressively took things further. At first, he convinced me to drink alcohol for the first time, then he exposed himself to me, and by the last night, he was more anxious to push things further.

At bedtime, he said it was important for us to sleep nude together, so that he could show me "what happened between a man and a woman." In a silent mantra, I repeated to myself over and over again, "please don't do anything – please don't do anything." The radio was on in the living room and the song "Yellow Bird" was playing. I zoned everything else out and listened intently to every word. Today, it can be playing softly in the background, but my mind will instantly pick up on it and take me momentarily back to that place.

It took a long while for the adrenalin to dissipate, and I laid there with a foreboding sense of dread about the future. Sleep finally came, but it was soon interrupted as I awoke to him repeatedly saying my name in a loud whisper, telling me to wake up. There was incessant rapping on our cabin door.

I was confused and groggy and did not know how to respond at first. He had hurriedly put some clothes on, and I lay there in the bedroom waiting to find out why someone was at the door in the middle of the night. As I listened to what sounded like agitation coming from several voices, I began to understand that I was hearing the sound of my own mother's voice. I could not compute this. I wondered if I might even be dreaming.

After a few moments, she stormed into the bedroom with a notable air of authority. And, even though I was covered up to my neck, she knew I was not clothed. As we both processed the shock of what each of us was seeing, she quietly asked me if I was afraid of the person in the next room. With tears streaming down my face, I shook my head, yes.

My mother had felt an absolute certainty in her gut that day, that something was wrong. With no money, she borrowed what she could, and took the train to the town where I was living, and then made her way to our foster home very late at night. Upon hearing I was at the lake with my foster dad, my mother issued an ultimatum – *take me there now or I will ask the police.*

My foster mother called a cab and they drove the 40 miles to the lake where my mom found me. It was one of the most helpless episodes of my life, and she was there to save me, all because she listened to her unwavering intuition about needing to be there that day.

She rescued me, at a time when she had given up her parental authority, and had no financial resources. The gratitude I have for my mom and how she listened to her intuition is profound.

MEET SHERRI

Sherri is an Anishinabe woman and a member of Yellow Quill First Nation in Saskatchewan. She is a survivor of the "Sixties Scoop", growing up in seven foster homes. After returning to university as a mature student, Sherri obtained both her undergraduate and graduate degrees at the University of Saskatchewan.

She has taught at both the First Nations University of Canada and the University of Saskatchewan as a Sessional Lecturer teaching a variety of Indigenous Studies classes, and working on curriculum development.

She is also a speaker and presenter, focusing on Indigenous history in Canada, as well as issues related to Child Welfare.

She is currently revising a completed manuscript about her experiences growing up in the foster care system and as an intergenerational survivor of the residential school system. She anticipates publication of her book in the summer or fall of 2019.

Personal photograph

She is married with three adult children, and has five grandchildren who are the absolute lights of her life.

Should you wish to connect with Sherri, you can reach her at: sherriswid@sasktel.net.

3

WRITTEN IN THE STARS

NICOLENE WATSON

"Tough times in life are designed to strengthen us and provide lessons to help us achieve the life we want, and deserve. When you can find acceptance and trust your inner voice in the midst of a storm, you make way for the sun."

NICOLENE'S STORY

Do you remember believing in Santa, longing for a particular 'gift' you so desperately wanted him to bring you? You hoped that gift would be waiting for you Christmas morning if you did everything right and behaved as best as you could. Each year you prayed that your special gift would finally arrive. Despite all the other wonderful gifts you received, the one you wanted more than anything, never came. To make matters worse, all of your friends got the gift you wanted, even those who hadn't asked for it! You wondered what you had done wrong, or if you were being punished. Why didn't Santa see how hard you worked or believe that you deserved it too?

This was my eleven year old niece's interpretation to me of what my husband and I were going through year after year, with the gift being a baby. She was the first person who had no experience with infertility, yet was able to express an empathetic understanding of our situation.

When I was 16, I no longer believed in Santa, but I sure believed in love. I daydreamed about my future husband; my knight in shining armour. I imagined our children playing out the kitchen window as I washed up the day's dishes. My husband would lean in from behind to wrap me tightly in his arms as he lovingly pecked me on the cheek with sincere admiration and gratitude for the family we created inside our white picket fence.

By the time I was 32 I had kissed my fair share of frogs before finally meeting my knight. He was the man from my daydreams, and would be the father of my children. We married four years later, and decided to start our family after one year as husband and wife. Just as planned, we got pregnant. It was exactly how I pictured my happily ever after.

Never did I imagine that we would only see our baby through the ultrasound where we saw a heart, but no heartbeat. We went on to lose our second baby and then our third, which almost brought me to my breaking point. Eventually we mustered up the courage to try again only to lose our fourth IVF (in vitro fertilization) baby, and our fifth and final baby all in the first three years of marriage.

During that time, we tried every treatment and test available to find an explanation. There was no medication, supplement, diet, or alternative therapy we didn't try on our quest for a family. In the end we were given a diagnosis of unexplained infertility and were in debt up to our eyeballs. Infertility treatments cost the equivalent of a down payment on a house, with no guarantees, or refunds.

Even though treatment left us with empty arms, the stressors from infertility forced us to change our mindset, and surround ourselves with positivity and happiness as best we could. On our wedding day we vowed that as long as we were together there was nothing we couldn't conquer.

My husband and I, together with our friend, created a fertility support group called YANA. We chose this name as an acronym for You Are Not Alone, because we needed to find other men and women to talk to who were also feeling isolated and alone. We recognized that unless you have walked the desperate road of infertility, it was impossible to relate to those who have. After three years it was clear that we needed support from others who understood what we were going through every month.

After we facilitated our first meeting, and heard some of the other women speak about the same deep, emotional pain that I was going through, my husband realized he wasn't supporting me to the best of his abilities. Hearing other women speak helped him realize what I was going through was normal. Little did we know that by going public about our infertility that we would not only become stronger as a couple, but more importantly, that we would be approached by a stranger and asked to adopt a baby from Nunavut.

Call it fate or a gift from the Universe, but if there were ever something written in the stars for me, it was to be a mother. After sixty months of trying, we were ready to accept life without children. Surprisingly, nine months later the next chapter of our lives found us experiencing the joys of parenthood making every attempt and loss worthwhile.

Our journey from diagnosed unexplained infertility to adoption is certainly unlike most. We were chosen for private adoption two months before the due date, so I immediately hired an adoption lawyer and social worker. However, only four days later, the birth Grandma called and said that our baby was coming. We were in complete shock. Our 3lb 8ounce baby entered the world in Nunavut at 31 weeks gestation, and was on her way to the NICU in Winnipeg by medevac. Within the hour our car was packed and we drove all night to meet our baby.

Words cannot describe the feeling of meeting our daughter, who we named Lola, and also how memorable it was to spend a week with our baby's birth mom and grandma. We shared as much laughter as tears in our short time together while the adoption legalities were being prepared. When it was time for them to return to Nunavut we didn't say goodbye, we said see you soon. Not only did we gain a child, but also a new culture and family.

I spent the next two weeks caring for Lola while working with the doctors to find a way to get us transferred home. Meanwhile, my husband was in Saskatoon keeping our company running. None of the provinces involved would cover travel costs, but I trusted my intuition and stayed focused on our miracle baby knowing the stars would align. Then it happened. A fellow NICU mom overheard our story and introduced me to *Jordan's Principal*, a fund developed in Canada to ensure that First Nations and Inuit children have equitable access to all government-funded services. Because we were able to access this for Lola, we received $23,000 for our medevac transfer home.

Our infertility journey allowed me to understand wholeheartedly that tough times in life are designed to strengthen us and to face hardships with confidence. My intense desire to be a mom that I've had since my late teens, was indisputably my intuition's way of telling me to trust that it would happen, maybe just not how I expected.

Now as parents, after six years of failed infertility treatments, we can reflect on what our bundle of joy has brought to our world. Our journey to a family of three had a purpose and we would not change a thing. For me, I finally feel like myself. Being a mom, I feel like I am the person I was always meant to be. If you ask Ryan what his favourite thing about being a parent is so far, he will tell you it is watching me experience motherhood.

FIRESIDE CHAT

As a young girl, I knew Nicolene and her family through swimming. Having had two children myself with medical assistance, I had spoken at YANA and reconnected with Nicolene after many years. One thing I have learned over the years is how vastly alike and different the experiences can be as people try to begin their families. Nicolene kind of "secretly disappeared" and then reappeared with the story of Lola, so I am eager to learn more!

What are the top three lessons you have learned from this experience and how do they impact how you live now?

I'll never forget the day my husband lost his wedding ring and I was sick about it. The problem was, I was sure I had moved it to a safer location, but could not remember where so I blamed myself. I was on my hands and knees throughout our entire house. I even looked in the freezer!

The next day, my morning meditation's lesson was to *accept what is, just as it is, in each and every moment*. I recall comparing my obsession to find his ring much like trying to find an explanation for why I couldn't sustain a pregnancy. In that moment I realized that I had to let go of finding this ring, just as much as I had to let go of the need to control my fertility. I had to detach from our monthly treatments and failures, and believe that our journey had a purpose. The day after this revelation I found his ring.

To this day I practice *giving up my need for control*

especially now that I'm a mother. If I allowed control to take over, I'd end up feeling responsible for everything and carry the burden of resentment. I'm ready for life's challenges and approach them now as lessons to strengthen the woman I've become.

Because of my infertility struggles I understand that *boundaries* are healthy and crucial to maintain the life I want, and I no longer carry guilt over setting them. Infertility is a roller coaster ride of emotions, so by creating boundaries I made space for a much smoother ride.

We all face challenges in life whether it be the loss of fertility, our health or our children's, the loss of a job, our home, our marriage or parents, etc. Knowing what's around the corner is impossible to predict. We must listen to that inner voice, and trust that everything has a way of working out.

Today I choose to live each day as if it were my last inspiring others to do the same along the way. We all have the power of choice, and happiness is what I choose.

What was the "pivot point" in this experience where things began to change for you in

terms of how you thought and felt about your situation? How did your thoughts and feelings change and how did that change impact the outcome?

Can you share them with us?

For three years my diagnosis of unexplained infertility was my biggest kept secret. Only a handful of people knew about our five lost babies, and monthly fertility treatment. My relationships were becoming strained or nonexistent the longer our treatments went on. People didn't know what to say or worse yet, said things that only caused more hurt. Just as my journey's wounds would start to heal, they were ripped open again with another failed cycle.

I watched women around me become pregnant, some without even trying. I was jealous when I knew I should be happy. I wanted more than anything in this world to be someone's mommy. What was wrong with me? What was wrong with us? Why didn't people get how I was feeling?

At the beginning of our journey I suppressed my pain hoping that once I could sustain a pregnancy that it would all go away, but by the fourth year I was at my breaking point. After our fifth loss I could no longer ignore the voice inside me saying "speak your truth to others who get it." And so I did. I was tired of faking it and putting everyone else's needs ahead of my own. Moms, baby bumps, and families were everywhere. It was clear that what I was doing wasn't working and I understood that if I wanted a different outcome I had to change.

Weeks following, as fate would have it, there she was. I found my person. Talking with her gave me a sense of normalcy in a world full of mom clubs. She too was determined to find a better support system and presented me with the opportunity of starting a monthly support group. I was never more terrified about "coming out" to the world, yet at the same time, I wanted to scream our story from the rooftops. It was time to choose me and put my needs first regardless of being judged or caring what anyone thought.

Within a week I had written our website, introduced our cause on social media, and hit the streets with posters in hand. Our first meeting was in January of 2016 – four years after our journey began. I was no longer in isolation, and finally felt I could lower my expectations of others because I found my tribe in YANA. I was free from the shackles of feeling alone on my journey but more importantly, I was able to see how strong and courageous I had become because of our infertility.

I soon learned that coming out to the world was going to get harder before it got easier. But in the end, it was the best decision I could have made, and definitely became a pivot point in my journey.

What was the worst advice people gave you or the most annoying things that people said to you when you were in the deepest point of suffering. Explain?

I think the worst experiences that came from people was their lack of acknowledging what we were going through at the time, and their lack of empathy *especially* after going public with our struggles. It was hard when people showed a disinterest towards what treatment I was undergoing at the time, or the surgery that was next in attempt to find answers, but who could blame them,

I suppose. I kept telling myself that everyone has struggles and busy schedules, which became my motivation to find others on the same road as us.

I do understand that the beginning of my journey was spent mostly in silence by choice, which didn't help my sense of isolation, however when I did muster up the courage and confidence to come out from under the 'veil of infertility' the support was still lacking despite my efforts of trying to educating them by sharing articles on "what to say, and what not to say" or 'how to support a loved one through infertility". If they weren't going to ask what I needed in terms of support, I was going to tell them. I came to accept that those who cared would stay by my side.

Having six years of experience with infertility, and over two years of Co-Facilitating Saskatoon's fertility support group, some common examples of *what not to say* to someone experiencing infertility are:

- *Trust me, you're lucky you don't have kids.*
- *You need to relax and go on a vacation. All your stress is causing your infertility and your*

mind is probably preventing you from conceiving.
- *Maybe you're not meant to be a parent. You should just get over it.*
- *You have plenty of time, or you shouldn't have waited so long.*
- *Whose fault is it, yours or his?*
- *It could be worse, you could have cancer.*

If you want to be supportive to friends and family facing a crisis educate yourself on why the above statements are inappropriate and keep in mind, it's often helpful to do more listening than speaking.

What is your advice to family and friends of people who are facing infertility?

Respect boundaries. Some people prefer their privacy and others choose to be open. In our case we experienced both scenarios so it's best to ask the couple for ways you can show your support.

Keep the lines of communication open and do not hide pregnancy announcements from them, however, be tactful when doing so. Find out beforehand how they would prefer to hear the news *before* a possible pregnancy happens. If someone in their circle becomes pregnant protect them by letting them know you are thinking of them, and understand how other people's pregnancies are triggers when experiencing failed cycles every month.

Value them in your family unit. Infertility will become part of your family's history so how you chose to adapt and cope with their journey will play a huge factor in the future. Be sensitive to their needs particularly around family gatherings where babies and children are involved and respect their decision if they do not attend. Continue to encourage their involvement especially if their journey ends without children. Whether this happens or not realize the importance of their relationship with your children.

Empathize with their pain and the pressure from possibly never having children of their own. Acknowledge their stress and situation by asking them what they need. Even though it might be difficult to know what to say, admit this to them rather than saying nothing at all. Recognize that most holidays can be difficult especially if they have miscarried since most holidays emphasize children, which is a reminder of the loss of motherhood. Send tokens of kindness in remembrance of losses or failed treatments whether through a text, email or by mail, arrange meals, help them with chores or drop off their favourite treat. Acts of service and empathy for what they're experiencing goes a long way.

Infertility is an emotional and medical crisis, so acknowledge this. If you don't you are only minimizing their involuntary ability to have children, their emotional and physical pain, financial and marital strain, failed monthly attempts, testing and surgeries that accompany infertility. Avoid blame and rigid expectations, but rather, be sensitive to their pain and inability to expand their family.

How has intuition served you on your journey? We often discount the intelligence that our "gut feeling" has - how has it served you?

Five years after our first miscarriage it was time to face our final treatment with the outcome of either becoming a mother, or not. Either way I was ready. By this point I had gained full trust in the fact that our journey had a purpose, I just didn't know what that was yet.

Three years earlier, as our last resort, we adopted three embryos from the only woman I connected with at our fertility clinic during IVF. As fate would have it, she was a nurse to my mom during chemotherapy. To me this was proof that my mom, my angel, was watching over me.

December was spent preparing my body for the adopted embryo transfer with the use of hormone injections, medications and alternative therapies. Just before Christmas our results were in and our embryo failed to implant. I experienced the longest exhale of my life. It was over. We had spent five years out of the six that we were married trying to have a baby, and we didn't have to do it anymore.

To mine and my husband's surprise I wasted no time, and with dry eyes I got right up and spent the rest of the day clearing out our lifeless baby room and transformed it into my very own 'zen den'! My mental preparation and tough choices had paid off, and I felt surprisingly calm. I had complete faith in the unknown, and for the first time, it was time to do me.

I trusted that our journey had a purpose and had

faith in the fact that I was on the right path regardless of the outcome of our fertility journey. Practicing meditation and positivity, along with creating a support system through YANA, sharing our story, and listening to my gut feelings allowed me to see with confidence that where I was at this point in my life was right where I was meant to be.

Nine months later by sharing our story, we were chosen for private adoption, and our baby was finally in my arms. I was somebody's mom!

MEET NICOLENE

Nicolene was born on December 27th 1974 in Saskatoon Saskatchewan. She spent her early working years primarily in the beauty industry, as well as held positions in larger corporations.

She, along with her siblings, organize an annual triathlon on Mother's Day in memory of their mom and proceeds from the race support various local charities.

She is the co-founder of YANA, a fertility support group in Saskatoon. She has written about her infertility journey in Vintage Gypsy Magazine, and REFINED Magazine, and she hopes to write her story as a book in the future. Today Nicolene manages all media, advertising, human resources and finances for an award winning Masonry Company, Rocco Masons Corporation, where she works with her husband, Ryan.

For more about Nicolene, go to yanasaskatoon.weebly.com and roccomasons.com.

You can email her directly at: nicolene@roccomasons.com.

Photo Credit: Emma Love Photography

Backcover Photo Credit: Ryan Watson

4

FROM GRIEF TO GRATITUDE

CAROLYN S. SCHRADER

"I believe that Grief is a working state of being, that allows us to find the emotional tools to help maneuver through the pain and sadness of our losses, and find the best way in moving forward with our life."

CAROLYN'S STORY

Death tried, multiple times, to bring me to my knees. Every time I lost a loved one, death put my mental and emotional ability to survive to the test. It is by the grace of my faith, keeping love alive, hanging onto hope, having the will to forgive, and practicing gratitude, that I can say that death did not succeed. Instead, my experiences with death taught me many lessons and showed me how practicing gratitude could help me navigate through my grief.

Early in our marriage, my husband Jim and I plummeted into hell with the devastating loss of our seventeen-month-old twin boys, Travis and Tyson. It was accidental carbon monoxide poisoning, and we raced against time to save them. They were medevaced to the hospital. The emergency room filled with doctors and nurses fighting to keep our beautiful little sons alive. Tyson did not make it through the night. I held him and loved him until the coroner came. Just before they took him from my arms, I felt his soul leave his earthly body. Travis, plugged into a myriad of machines to keep him alive, showed no signs of brain activity by morning, and we had to make the unthinkable decision to take him off life support. Again, I held him close until the coroner came to take him to be with his brother, and I knew then as I did just a few moments earlier when my little boy's sweet soul left his body. Our boys came into our world together, and now they would transition from this life together. Their death changed everything about who Jim and I were, and who we were going to be. All traces of innocence were gone forever.

On May 15th, 2014, my husband called me at work and said he was going to drive out to his favorite golf course, located in a neighboring small town. We had a date night planned and, worried that he would be late, I asked him if he would play at a course closer to our home. He assured me that it would be okay and promised that he would be back with plenty of time.

I left work early so I could stop and visit our longtime friend in the hospital. Right after I arrived, their doctor came into his room and told our friend's wife and their daughters that her husband did not have much time left to live. I stayed with them until they could get ahold of other family members. We lost a dear friend just six months before and now this. I remember thinking that my husband would have a hard time handling this news and wondered how I would be able to tell him.

After making the stop on the way home from

work, I called my husband on the phone. There was no answer. I thought that he might be running late or he could be in the shower. I was halfway home when it donned on me that he had not called me to say he was on his way home. I was two blocks away from our home when I saw our driveway was empty. My heart started beating faster as I pulled into our driveway. I tried my husband again on his cell phone. No answer. My panic started to rise, but I fought against it to remain calm.

As I went in our home, I kept telling myself that my husband would be pulling into the driveway any moment. I tried to convince myself that he forgot his phone charger and his phone was dead.

Then it came. A loud, heavy knock banged on our front door. I moved the curtain aside and saw a man standing at my door. A man, who was wearing a uniform. The minute I got the door open, the police officer asked if I was Carolyn Schrader, but without answering, I interrupted. *Is this about my husband? Has he been in an accident? Is he ok?*

My heart felt like it was pounding out of my chest.

And then -

Mrs. Shrader, your husband is dead. He died on the golf course.

Just like that. *Your husband is dead.*

I was fighting to comprehend what he was saying. The officer asked me if I was alone and who he should call. I could not think. He asked me again. Our son. I had to call our son and tell him his father was dead. I was shaking so much that when my son answered, I could not speak. The officer took my phone and told him the news.

With the evening closing in, confusion, shock, and pain came and went as my mind raced from tragedy to tragedy. I recalled all of the losses I had experienced that were sudden and without warning: My great-grandparents, grandparents, parents, aunts, uncles, cousins, unborn sibling, one of my best girlfriends, a co-worker, parents-in-law, sister-in-law, two of my husband's close friends, a miscarriage, our twin boys, and now my husband of forty-six years. My head was reeling; my heart once again broke into pieces, and I knew this was only the beginning of yet another grief-laden path through which I had to walk.

Even though every experience with death that I have had so far has brought me unthinkable shock, pain, sadness, and grief, I have maintained a sense of gratitude for the lives that I lost. This overwhelming feeling of gratitude has been an essential tool that has helped me cope and fight against the power that death has tried to have over me.

FIRESIDE CHAT

Carolyn and I have "known one another" in the online space for many years. I recall the day she posted on Facebook that her husband had passed away suddenly. She is also one of my clients, and although Carolyn had just completed her own book on grief, I knew there was so much more to her story. I invited her to be a part of INSPIRED LIVING. She graciously accepted. Carolyn and I sit down to discuss the lessons and wisdom she has pulled from the grief she has experienced throughout her lifetime.

What are the most important lessons have you learned about gratitude that you apply to how you live your life after experiencing so much loss?

My experiences have taught me the importance of finding gratitude while going through grief. I know the importance of appreciating the lives of my loved ones and the time I had with them no matter how long or short. I have been reminded by each loss that we are on this earth for a very short time, and that time is determined by a force outside of our control.

Gratitude and forgiveness can be difficult to practice in times of shock, pain and immense sadness. If I had not concentrated on feeling gratitude for the love, antics, and experiences we had with our twins, I would not have made it through the intense pain of losing them.

Our loss of our little boys was our worst nightmare, and learning how to pick up the pieces of our life afterwards was difficult. For all it took from us and for all it taught us, I am fortunate to be able to help others who have experienced loss of a loved one to discover their own tools that will help them on their unique journey.

I have learned that there is no answer to the question of why. I learned this lesson many times when our twins died. I no longer ask why, as the lack of response only brings anger and frustration. I now ask *how*. How can I get through the pain and stay stable?

When you were facing the most difficult point in your journey, what was the most challenging decision you had to make and why?

I believe that as difficult as each loss in my life was, that to this day the most challenging decision we had to make was to allow the doctors to take our Travis off of life support. This was a decision we had to make during the most devastating time in our lives. We went from selfishly saying *no, please we have to keep him with us,* to finally accepting that it was best for us to let him go on his own. He left us very quickly, and we knew it was the right decision, albeit the hardest, for all of us. This was the ultimate lesson in "letting go" for the sake of another. For their final time on this earth, we had them placed together in one casket, to be together for their journey to their next destination.

After my husband died, I had to make a decision that I did not anticipate. While we were trying to get our hearts and heads around the fact that he was gone, and never coming home again, my phone rang. It was at about 11:30 pm and on the other end of the line was a "life-giving" organization. They said since my husband did not have a donor's approval on his driver license would I be willing to give consent to donate any of his organs that could help others. I cannot even begin to describe what that call did to my son and me. It was one more lesson of letting go for the sake of others. Together we decided to donate any of the organs that would help other people to continue living their lives.

What would you do differently if you were to find yourself experiencing this "event" again as your much wiser self?

All of my life I have heard that hindsight is 20/20; however, from experience, I can also say that hindsight is one of the most valuable teaching tools. When we go into the hindsight zone about a particular event in our life, we often view it as a negative using phrases like "should have", and it's common to beat ourselves up a bit, or a lot, depending on how serious the "should have" is to us. We often wished we had done things differently than what we did at the time of the event or we become uncomfortable with how we handled the event and we relive the pain all over again. The hindsight lesson I learned, or what I would do differently if I experience these losses in the future, is that grief is personal, and I will not allow others to dictate how long I grieve, or the way I need to grieve. I will not allow someone else's perception of who they think I am, to override who I know myself to be. I have always known that keeping grief buried within one's emotional vaults could be damaging both to our health and emotional wellness. In my case, because I have had to be a survivor of negative life situations from birth, I instinctively invented ways to get me through without falling into the depths of no return. I now use the advantages of hindsight as a healing tool for myself and to help others. I have looked back at my life and in every case where there was a reason to say "I should have," it involved allowing someone else's opinions to become more valid than mine.

Bottom line; Whoever gives you advice, respectively give them their due consideration to what they say, then only keep that which fits well within the directions you want to go, what supports the decisions you want to make, and fits into your value system, leaving the rest behind.

What is your advice to people who are struggling with the same experience you have lived through?

I make it a practice never to give advice. However, I do offer guidance and clarity to help with the journey through grief. Losing a loved one to death is a harsh, devastating, and long-term reality. The first thing I would tell someone who has gone through a similar experience is that I have found grief to be a bridge for getting to the other side of pain, and intense sadness, to a more livable state of being. The second thing I would share with someone going through a similar experience is that it is imperative to establish friendships with people who will stay with you amidst life's trials and devastations. My best friend of over 40 years has been through her own losses, and she gets it. We support each other and make sure we do not disappear into the bowels of hell never to return. When my husband passed away, she gave me a month of side-by-side comfort, cried with me and gave me added strength to begin my long walk. Then one day she called me and said, "Ok Missy Diva Queen, time to straighten your crown, get dressed and get out!" It was just what I needed. I got up, got dressed, straightened my emotional crown and started my journey to figuring out who I was going to be. Find that friend or group of friends who you can count on to lay out the nets that will catch you when you start falling. Those who will pick you up, set you on your feet, and give you the strength and encouragement to keep on keeping on.

What was the "pivot point" in this experience where things began to change for you in terms of how you thought and felt about your situation? How did your thoughts and feelings change and how did that change impact the outcome?

My pivot points came after I allowed myself to grieve each loss. I would finally let myself cry if the emotion called the tears forward. After, as I sat alone with no more tears to fall, I had a "what the hell do I do now" moment. I found that in these moments, I saw grief as a bridge scattered with potholes of shock, anger, pain, and sadness. It was in these moments that I realized that the only way to get across the bridge without falling into the holes, and thus landing in the pits of despair and depression, was to fill them with gratitude and positive memories of each person's life. A strategy that has helped in these pivot points is one that I learned as a Life Coach and Grief Mentor. I use life mapping and vision boards to move forward to positive outcomes. I start with a piece of paper, and I draw a bridge.

The first bridge was for my husband. I drew circles on it that represented potholes and labeled them with my feelings and emotions. The first ones were regrets, unforgiveness, anger, and sadness for all of the things we were not able to do together. I listed everything that brought me tears and pain. Then I labeled some with what I knew I would miss the most. I studied this drawing for quite some time that evening trying to figure out how this could help me navigate through my grief, and the thought finally came to me to fill each pothole with a counter memory of all we had done together. This was allowing me to cross over from the harshness of my loss and find a way to begin moving forward. I wanted to remember my husband for the happiness we shared and not for the shock and pain of his death. I did not want to dwell on the memories of wasted time together or being angry for the times we allowed our egos to get in our way. My little boy's bridge had only one negative pothole that represented all that would never be. For now, I have written I am grateful for the time they were loaned to us and for all they gave us and taught us. This process has brought an outcome of giving me the strength to keep on moving through life and making the most of my moments.

What are the top three lessons you have learned from this experience and how do they impact how you live now?

At the top of my list of things I have learned, from the losses in my life, has been to think about grief as a time to sort through the pain.

Grief is a bridge to managing the shock, pain, and sadness brought about from the death of a loved one or an ending to a life event.

If I was asked what I would like others to learn from my experiences, it is that we need to think differently about grief and how to recognize our pain. We need to give grief the respect and time it needs to help move us forward through our losses. To learn, that the onset of the emotional state of grief is our protection and is the key to our rebuilding and finding our way out of the depths of despair. We never "get over" grief; we only "get through" grief. The period for grieving is very different for each person, and being in mourning provides time to pay respect in an open way.

It is so important to be present in every aspect of your life and with every relationship.

The old saying of stop and smell the roses is a simple directive for living a balanced life. One of the many things the death of my little boys and my husband has taught me is to "stop and smell the roses." To stop rushing about and being so busy and instead, be present in everything. To be present when someone is talking; to see them, hear them and acknowledge what they have to say, their opinions and how they feel. When I am out in nature, I pay more attention to all there is to see. I am now "present" more than I have ever been.

The importance of staying in a constant state of gratitude.

From my childhood to just before my husband died, I was in the habit of exchanging my grief with thoughts of the happy times I had with loved ones who passed away. I would think about the positive reasons for having them in my life to keep my emotions under control and not upset anyone else. The minute I open my eyes, I say Thank you. I say little prayers of gratitude all day long and then again at night before I go to sleep. I acknowledge how grateful I am for having time to walk through this life, how grateful I am for my family, and the beautiful, loving friends I have, no matter how long the relationship lasts. When we are thankful, it is difficult to be negative. And so, I fully believe gratitude to be a central component to living a happy life.

How has intuition served you on your journey? We often discount the intelligence that our "gut feeling" has - how has it served you?

From early childhood, I have had a strong intuitive gift. I never gave it much thought, as it was natural for me. Being openly intuitive ran in my family on my Dad's side, and my birth mother was Native American. Intuitive guidance is the way of her people. When I got married, my intuitive abilities bothered my husband a great deal. My ability to "know stuff" that he could find no logical reason for made him nervous. He understood "gut instinct" but not the "knowing" that went with my "gut instinct." I began to override my intuition, and when I would allow it, I certainly did not express it. Even when it came as a warning, I would tell myself to stop being wary of things and be braver. It was after my husband passed away and I had my night of reckoning that I realized that the one constant, in each life event, was that I had a knowing, a warning or guidance that I should have heeded. The day my husband died, I was uneasy all day. When he called me to tell me he was going to his favorite golf course in another town, which was nothing unusual, I immediately felt ill at ease about it, and even though I asked him to go closer to home, I did not want to tell him I felt uneasy about it. Our intuitions are a gift of protection, forewarning, and insight. Our Intuition is our natural warning and guidance system for making right or safer decisions for ourselves, and many times, for those closest to us. Sadly, one of the hardest lessons about not trusting my intuition came when my husband passed away. I wonder "IF" I had listened to my intuition and insisted that my husband not go that far away to golf if his transition would have been different. Maybe I would have been able to get to him quickly and to hold him and love him as his heart and soul left this life. I believe that listening and trusting our intuition can, in many cases, cancel the proverbial "If."

MEET CAROLYN

Carolyn (Carrie) Schrader is a Certified Professional Life, NLP and Grief Coach. Carolyn's losses have been enormous. She has gone through the death of two beautiful children, her husband, grandparents, parents, aunts, uncles, cousins, siblings, many extended family members, friends and pets. She has also experienced personal health losses, jobs, homes, dreams, possibilities, relationships and at times the loss of who she was as a person. She has lived in Missouri, Washington, Oregon, Alaska, New Hampshire and now California. She grew up in a hardworking, blue-collar family.

Carolyn enjoyed many careers in her over 50

years of work life. She held a License in Cosmetology for over 50 years, performed as a Radio Announcer, (going on air with the moniker "Scout") with her husband, and worked as a Continuity Director, Copy Writer, and Radio Advertising sales, worked in Human Resources, for many branches of the Military, served as Office Manager and Deputy Director/Chief Financial Officer for the Armed Services YMCA of Alaska. She retired in 2014 as the Family Assistance Coordinator/Life Coach for the Alaska National Guard.

She holds an AA in Psychology, Certification for Professional Life, Grief and NLP Coaching, Grief Responder, Certified Crisis Responder, Suicide Responder, Victims Advocate, and Certified Emergency Preparedness Trainer. Carolyn is an Author, Writer, Blogger, Published Columnist, Teacher/Trainer and Public Speaker.

Photo Credit: Michael Haddad Photography

Connect with Carolyn:

- Her book, ***Death Did Us Part: Stories of Grief and Gratitude*** is available on Amazon in paperback and Kindle format.
- Email: carolyn@carolynschrader.net
- Website: carolynschrader.net

5

UNSHAKABLE LOVE

ROBIN HILTON

"When you love your body, you open yourself to fully allow the joy that your one, magical life has to offer."

ROBIN'S STORY

I stood at the top of the mountain, arms raised to the sky, light rain falling on my skin and tears streaming down my face. At this moment, I noticed something happening in my body that I had been trying for years to articulate. This is what it felt like to be fully alive, present, embodied, and completely immersed in the world that surrounded me. Standing there, I felt ready to step into life with a new knowing, and understanding. It is through this knowing that I would eventually learn a kind of self-love I never thought possible. I call this kind of love, *unshakable love*.

The pivotal moment on the mountain happened at Wanderlust Yoga Festival in Whistler, British Columbia, in 2012. I ventured up the mountain, defying my fear of heights, to attend a yoga class.

I left the mountain that day with the essential truth of yoga as an embodied knowing - and a deeper appreciation for how my experience on the mat influences how I move through my life off the mat. I experienced the feeling of being fully enraptured in a single moment, transcending time and space. I also gained a blueprint for how I could experience life in that same way as I had in that class.

The instructor's guidance on the mountain emphasized slow, body aware transitions, and invited complete embodiment. The full expression of the postures represent the significant moments in life like births, graduations, and weddings. The space between the postures represent the rest of life. The seemingly mundane day-to-day experiences like going to work, walking the kids to school, or making dinner. Both the full expression and the space between each pose is important, but through this new understanding, my focus changed to the everyday life that happens between the moments of expansion.

The connection between practicing yoga on and off the mat became central to sharing yoga with other women as a tool for living a fulfilled life. My newfound appreciation for everyday life foreshadowed my later discovery of *Tantra* and the philosophical and spiritual tradition that sees Divinity in all aspects of life. Studying *Tantra* helped me achieve a deeper purpose to my work because I wanted my clients to know the bliss available to them in the ordinary moments of life.

The time between the mountaintop and discovering *Tantra* was a rich battleground for the clashing energies of my deeply ingrained and destructive habits from my past, and a new understanding that was awakening within me. Those years were not without drama, mistakes, tough decisions and big realizations.

I believe that the greatest teachers are those who have done things the hard way. I count myself as someone who has learned hard lessons, made huge mistakes, tried everything, and yet, I kept going. My path lead me to a concept that I call *unshakable love*, and my life's purpose is to share this with women, so that their journey to loving themselves, their bodies, and their lives feels less tumultuous and more pleasurable than it was for me.

I want all women to know that it is possible to look in the mirror and feel their hearts expand with pure love because all they can see is true radiance, and to know that it is possible to get past wherever they feel they are at right now so that they can get to where they want to go.

It's possible, because I did it.

FIRESIDE CHAT

I met Robin online and attended one of her introductory workshops. I loved her energy and approach to topics that mattered to me because I fully acknowledge that people all heal differently. While at the workshop, she led me in a meditation that had me totally forgetting where or who I was, startled to return to my own body in a room full of people I didn't know. I am honoured to learn more about her through INSPIRED LIVING.

What are the key factors to healing you from your negative experiences?

Looking back, I can clearly see that the key factors that healed me from my negative experiences were learning to practice and teach yoga, the realization that the present moment is a place where I can experience gratitude, bliss, magic and awe and finally, the recognition that pleasure can be a powerful healing tool.

Who would have thought that showing up for my first yoga class over eleven years ago with my two youngest daughters in tow would completely transform my life. Before yoga, I was anxious and stuck in a world of stressful thoughts and disconnection with my body. I would not say yoga is the end of my healing journey, but it was the entry point that I needed at the time.

Yoga offered me a new career and a new outlook

on life. It also brought me to the top of Whistler Mountain for what I see now was a flash of enlightened knowing. I realized as I gazed up at the cloudy sky, raindrops falling on my face, that there was a deeper truth to life and that serendipity is always unfolding around me. I recognized the sheer beauty of human existence and knew that it was crucial that I continue to deepen this understanding so I could fully experience the magic of living.

After Whistler, my life changed dramatically. I left the yoga studio where I worked and practiced, and relocated to a small community. I opened my own studio, and developed my unique teaching style. Shortly after moving, I read Eckhart Tolle's book, *A New Earth,* and found myself understanding what had happened to me on the mountain that day. A moment of complete and total presence that evaporated all stress and worry. I knew that I wanted to feel this way more often and share that information with others.

About a year after opening the studio, I found myself overworked and struggled to keep up with all of the responsibilities I had taken on. I noticed that I was feeling more and more disconnected from my passion. In the midst of burnout, I attended a *Tantra* yoga retreat. One evening during the retreat, I was browsing the internet, and came upon my teacher, Layla Martin. Layla combines *Tantra*, Jade Egg healing, and personal empowerment in her work to awaken women to the beauty and magic of their sexuality. I joined Layla's coaching program and began to work intimately with tools that opened me both emotionally and physically to the power contained within my body.

I learned how to use pleasure to heal shame, fear, and shutdown in my sexuality, to heal my childhood wounds around the need for external validation, and to heal the way I felt about my body. Learning how to use pleasure as a healing tool allowed me to develop unshakable love. Pleasure was and continues to be, a transformative and healing tool in my life.

What was the "pivot point" in this experience where things began to change for you in terms of how you thought and felt about your situation? How did your thoughts and feelings change and how did that change impact the outcome?

When I first discovered *Tantra*, I had no clue that it would eventually allow me to love my body and myself in a genuine way. My intention when I began practicing was to find more excitement in my life, and in the bedroom, and I wanted to experience an awakening of my sensuality and a deeper connection to my partner, and the world around me.

One of the first *Taoist Tantric* practices that I learned was breast massage, and it was not long after I began practicing it that I noticed my experience changing when I looked in the mirror. I began to love what I saw, and instead of criticizing my flaws I was able to see my beauty. At this point, I became a breast massage evangelist! I told every woman that I knew about this amazing healing practice. Little did I know that this was just the start of the body love transformation I would eventually have.

Over the next two years, I continued to work with awakening my sensuality, and opening myself to deeper experiences of pleasure and connection to my body. During the summer of 2018, I had the profound realization that a side effect of my dedication to *Tantric* practice was that I fell in love with my body.

Discovering *Tantra*, and the practice of breast massage changed a lot for me and all of those changes were challenged and validated when I replied to documentary photographer, Jamie Woytuik's model request. During this shoot, I waded into waist high water with the instruction to connect to my body and the way it was experiencing the sensations of the natural world. I dropped all of my inhibitions and allowed myself to be fully present in my body moving freely in the still, calm energy of the golden, early evening sun.

When I saw the photos, I was awestruck. As a woman who has traditionally considered herself non-photogenic, I saw beauty that I hadn't ever seen in myself before. It dawned on me that when I allowed myself to be fully present, fully embodied, and uninhibited I was also breathtakingly beautiful. I also knew that I had discovered something that had eluded me up until that point – it was at this time that I found unshakable body love and I also knew how to teach other women to do the same.

Being seen by Jamie and having what she saw reflect so perfectly in her art work allowed me to see how my soul shines when I let go of my inhibitions and allow my authenticity to beam through. I could now use the tools that I used to get there to teach other women. I could help them express the same feeling as I had felt, of knowing their beauty as an embodied truth.

If you had advice for your younger self, what would it be? Could this advice help you side step some suffering? If so, how?

The advice that I would give my younger self is, love yourself in every moment and that you are innately worthy of all the love you crave.

Like many women, I spent most of my life with the belief that validation for my worth had to come from outside of myself. I sought attention from teachers, my parents, friends, and boys, and continually felt the sting of pain when the unconditional love that I wanted did not happen in the way I wanted it to. I believed that praise, attention, and time meant that I was loved. I took this attention seeking behavior with me into my first-year of University where I partied more than I studied and attracted men who wanted to take advantage of my lack of self-worth.

In University, I studied feminism and graduated

with a Women's Studies degree but my continued disconnection with my body led to excessive drug and alcohol use that lasted until I discovered that I was pregnant with my first daughter at the age of 28. Self-care wasn't even on my radar during those years beyond maintaining a stylish outward appearance with clothing, hair, and makeup. I remember continually dieting, binging, and restricting food without any consideration for how my body actually felt. I suffered from extreme stomach pain when I was feeling anxious and was often sick or felt under the weather.

Pregnancy changed a lot for me because I was suddenly responsible for the care of a human other than myself and I knew that her well-being was dependent on my ability to take care of my body in a loving and nurturing way. I quit drinking and taking drugs, and began to nourish my body in preparation for her birth and breastfeeding.

Three pregnancies, and two babies later, I found myself in an exhausted post-pregnancy body. I started a home based sewing business while on maternity leave after my second daughter was born, but after the birth of my third daughter, I quit sewing and began to practice yoga, eventually training to teach.

Those years when my children were small, I experienced a self – awakening, which ultimately led to one of the most challenging experiences of my life. My partner and I had been struggling to connect for years and as we grew apart, I found myself seeking validation for my worth outside of our relationship. My partner asked me to consider working through things, but I didn't believe it was possible to be together and also feel good about myself. I broke things off and found myself heavily influenced by the opinions of others as I clumsily navigated my way through the single life.

Had I known that my joy, happiness, and capacity for self-love would never come from someone outside of myself and had I known the truth of who I was at that time, I would have trusted myself more. Even if I had still made the choice to end the relationship I would have used that time to heal instead of making choices that ultimately hurt my children and my partner. I lived with the shame of this experience for many years, even after my partner and I reunited and got married. It wasn't until I began to explore

Tantra and the deep emotional healing that was available through connecting to a sacred experience of pleasure that I would be able to heal, and also establish a profound sense of embodied trust in my own capacity for self-love, safety, and belonging.

I think we all wish we could go back and whisper in the ear of our sixteen-year-old selves. We would share the wisdom and the experience we have acquired through the years to save our younger selves from the inevitable pain and suffering they experienced because they did not realize there was another way. I also believe that my wisdom comes from my journey, and that everything that happened to me has made me the woman I am today.

How has intuition served you on your journey? We often discount the intelligence that our " gut feeling" has - how has it served you?

Every step that I have taken towards loving my body and finding my soul's purpose has come from an intuitive flash of knowing exactly what to do next. It is when I have made choices based in logic or were heavily influenced by others that

I found myself heading in a direction that took me further away from joy.

As I have connected more with my body, I have been able to trust my intuitive guidance because I can literally feel it. Prior to this realization, I had no clue that my body was always giving me information about my surroundings and the choices that I was making. Learning to trust the pulsation of joy that flows through me when I am aligned, and learning to ask for guidance from my inner self has opened up countless opportunities and connections that have supported my journey towards healing and growth.

I have made split second decisions based on intuition that have all come from trusting a deeper knowing that has flowed through me since I began connecting to my body through practicing yoga and eventually, Tantra. For example, leaving my original yoga teaching job, deciding to open a yoga studio, clicking a link to find my *Tantra* teacher online, applying for the training to become a coach, signing up for a transformative women's nudity retreat, creating events, and saying "yes" to life and business opportunities.

Tantra has deepened my capacity to tune in and

trust my intuition by inviting me to see the Divine nature of all things. I now believe that my desires are part of my soul's journey and trusting the nudges that push me towards them will always take me exactly where I need to go.

I struggle with distractions, so listening to intuition has been an essential tool to bringing me back on track when I have gone off course. Every time I find myself going away from my true desires, I remember to listen to my intuition. There is a distinct sensation and ease in my life when I listen to my intuition that is not only pleasurable but also incredibly productive.

I believe now, more than ever, that my intuition is stronger when I have a spiritual connection to my body and the world around me. As I deepen that connection, I also find that I become more aligned with ease, pleasure, and service in all areas of my life.

If you were deprived of all but one of your coping mechanisms, which one would you keep and why?

If I lost every coping mechanism except for one, I would keep conscious, controlled breathing. Every time I teach new students in my yoga classes, I tell them that the single most transformative thing they will do in their practice is learn how to breathe with awareness.

From a simple intentional sigh to powerful healing conscious connected breath work sessions, I know that if I only had one tool to help me manage my stress, overcome fear, relax, and heal, it would be my breath.

Using my breath, I was able to show up and teach my first yoga class with confidence even after having a rough start to my teacher training a few months earlier. On that first day of training, we had to introduce ourselves to the rest of the group and I recall being so nervous before I had to talk in front of my, soon to be, teaching peers. My heart was beating so fast and I could barely hear myself think as it got closer to my turn. I managed to get something out, but I recall worrying that I would never be able to teach yoga because I was too shy to speak in front of a group of people.

It was about six months later that I found myself sitting in that same studio waiting for the students to arrive for my first class. I remember trying to calm myself down and I recalled that my teacher said that longer, slower exhales are calming and relaxing. I took the next few moments to breathe before teaching and my whole body calmed down as I prepared to step into a career that would ultimately lead me to *Tantra* and unshakable body love.

What do you do when you feel overwhelmed?

When I am overwhelmed, it is usually because I am not in alignment. I have taken on too much, said "yes" when I should have said "no", or I am distracted from how I want to live and serve in this world.

Overwhelm is always a signal for me to rest and recalibrate. I start by organizing my office space and make sure I have not been ignoring my accounting or my overrun inbox. I will also look at my schedule and create some white space by canceling or changing things around and letting go of anything that is causing me stress, or resentment. I am learning that my "no" is a service to both others and myself. It becomes easier every time I say it.

The most important part of managing overwhelm for me is to check on my self-care practices. Have I been eating well, have I been moving my body, have I been getting outside? Generally, overwhelm comes when I am working too much. I am learning to listen to the subtle cues my body gives me before I become overwhelmed. This is a practice of having unshakable body love. I act lovingly towards my body when she tells me that I'm not taking care of her. Anxiety, self-doubt, comparing, and being distracted are all signs that I need to take a break and do something loving for my body. If I ignore the subtle signs, then I will be on track to overwhelm. If I ignore feeling overwhelmed, then burnout will soon follow.

My most common self-care practices are to get outside and go for a walk with my husband and my dog, do some gentle yoga, have a bath, spend time with my kids, go to a spin class, or do a *Tantric* practice that will soothe my nervous system. Ensuring that I take the time to take care of my body, my essence and my spirituality allows me to quickly soothe any feelings of anxiety of overwhelm that come up easily and with pleasure.

What are the top three lessons you have

learned from this experience and how do they impact how you live now?

I have learned that loving my body is not about pretending that everything is amazing and that I am never triggered by the world around me.

Loving my body is about having an intimate relationship with how I feel moment to moment and being in a deep state of appreciation for the wisdom, beauty, bliss, and power my body is capable of. It is also about knowing that my body is not the truth of who I am, and that I am much more than flesh and bones. I believe that I am Divinity having a human experience through my body. It is this understanding that allows me to be in continual service to my body by speaking kindly to her, lovingly taking care of her, and enjoying the magic she offers me every single day. This type of relationship with my body allows me to navigate a world that continually sends messages that I am not enough or that I should look a particular way in order to be accepted and loved. When you know the truth of who you are, it becomes impossible not to love yourself.

I spent a lot of my life judging, comparing and competing with other women. I think that it is a natural, and unfortunate, consequence of thousands of years of patriarchy for women to feel threatened by each other. Women separate themselves from other women by judging them externally before taking the opportunity to connect and share experiences with them. I have found, again and again, that when I take the time to get to know women there is more that connects us than separates us.

Purposefully connecting with other women and being in spaces where we can vulnerably share without judgment is a necessary component of our collective healing as women.

Listening to other women share their experiences reminds me that I am not alone. I believe that women are powerful when we gather. It is necessary to purposefully seek out or create spaces where we can let our guards down and share vulnerably and freely while also feeling unconditional love and support from other women. This is how we heal both individually and collectively.

Being intimately connected to our bodies and experiencing the wide range of pleasure that is available to us is a powerful healing force.

Entering a state of appreciation for our bodies can help us heal childhood wounds, trauma, relationship issues, lack of desire, and poor body image. I believe that everyone should know that while healing might be difficult at times, it is also deeply nourishing, and can even be even ecstatic.

My own sensual awakening through pleasure has healed deep shame, trauma, and my belief that my worth was something that was determined by others for me. My sensual awakening has given me a deep appreciation for my body that grounds me in a sense of gratitude for this opportunity to live here and now on this planet. Through pleasure, colours have become brighter, and the natural world more awe-inspiring than ever, my joy feels constant and my world feels alive, turned on and vibrant. Even my pain has taken on a new flavor as I recognize that pain is as much a part of my humanity as pleasure allowing for grace during difficult moments and patience as I move through challenges.

What is your advice to people who are struggling with the same experience you have lived through?

I speak to women every day who are struggling in some way to love their bodies. They have battled poor body image or weight gain, or they have had illnesses and health struggles that felt like their body was betraying them. These women feel deeply disconnected, unable to appreciate the beauty, magic, and power that is available to them through intimately connecting with their body.

This disconnection has a far-reaching impact on the lives of the women I work with much like it had on my own. From compulsively weighing myself to restricting food to continually comparing myself to other women, my obsession with external validation and believing my value was tied up in others' perceptions of me took over my life, eventually leading to the demise, and almost permanent loss, of the relationship with my partner.

Based on what my Body Love Coaching clients tell me, not having a loving relationship with their bodies causes my clients to hold back from living their lives fully. They do not go after the things they most desire, they hold back in social situations, they do not show up fully for what they want most in their lives and that, in turn, greatly affects their overall level of happiness and fulfilment. They are missing out on their own lives.

My advice for women who are feeling disconnected from their bodies, who look in the mirror and struggle to see anything they love, is to seek support. Support can come in many forms, and for me, it was in the form of sisterhood connections and one-on-one coaching.

When I began the sensual awakening through *Tantra* that would eventually lead to having unshakable body love, I sought out connections with other women both in person and online. I also had weekly check-ins with women where we freely expressed our celebrations, fears, and desires and held space for our partners to do the same. The unconditional love and support of sisterhood taught me that I am never alone and that we are not as different from each other as we think. Simply knowing that other women are going through similar struggles feels healing and validating.

Ultimately, all humans crave love, safety, and belonging. The work of unshakable body love is to cultivate that sense of love, safety and belonging as an inner truth. Finding a loving and supportive community is the first step. I believe it is essential to reach out for deeper levels of support to do the inner work required to heal. I chose to do this inner work through the practice of *Tantra* and I joined online courses and worked with coaches to transform my relationship with my body. Having support has been essential on my journey to unshakable love and I suggest that, the first step would be to seek support. First, the support of a loving community and then the support of a coach or therapist to help with the inner work required for lasting and meaningful change.

As I was finishing up writing this chapter, I felt that I needed more guidance to connect to the message that needed to come through my words. I sat in meditation and asked for a message and as I tuned in, images of women flashed through my awareness. Long haired maidens and African Queens reminding me of the changing and impermanent nature of our bodies.

Later that day, I went to visit my mom who, at the age of 76 has advanced dementia and has been living in a nursing home for the past two years. As I looked around at the residents who are all in the end stage of their lives, I was reminded of my own mortality.

I watched my mom fall asleep in her chair after she had finished her meal and a woman came to sit in the chair next to us. Her face was wrinkled and her eyes, which you could barely see, were loving and curious. She sat down and looked around without acknowledging me. She felt present and content and I found myself overwhelmed with a feeling of sadness because my heart knew that her life is almost over. Her quiet presence reminded me of my own impatience, distractibility, and anxiety and as she gently took in her surroundings it dawned on me that it was imperative that I choose to live fully right now.

Why do we spend so much time fixated on how our bodies look when we have such a short time in them? Why do we focus on what's wrong with our bodies instead of celebrating the pleasure, bliss, and joy they are capable of giving us? Why do we focus so much on our impermanent nature and forget about the timeless, unchanging truth that is our true nature?

Women (and men), please love yourself more.

This life is too short for anything else. Find some support, and get the help you need to overcome your body shame. You deserve to love yourself fully.

MEET ROBIN

Robin Hilton is an entrepreneur, yoga studio owner, coach, photographer, teacher, and facilitator. Her work and passions centre on allowing women to recognize the magic there is in the world and within themselves.

Born and raised on the Canadian prairies, Robin lives in Indian Head, Saskatchewan with her husband and three daughters. Thanks to the power of the internet, and technology, she works with women around the world, offering a supportive space to connect and thrive in sisterhood and love. You can keep up with Robin's ever-expanding work at www.robinjoy.ca.

Photo Credit: Jamie Woytiuk

Robin has curated a collection of her favourite practices for women who are struggling with lack of confidence, negative body image, overwhelm, stress, anxiety or burnout. These practices are an invitation to return to your body to replenish, heal and relax. This free five-day mini course is available here: www.robinjoy.ca/sootheandnourish.

Backcover Photo Credit: Melissa Chapman -White Lotus Studios

6

FROM THE WOMAN IN ME TO THE WOMAN IN YOU

DIMPLE MUKHERJEE

"It's very difficult to ask for help when you're fearful of being judged and I see that all the time. But when you don't ask for help, you risk feeling alienated at a time when you need support the most. And you also risk staying in a situation, which no longer serves you."

DIMPLE'S STORY

The bedroom looked clear and safe. Beckoning and taunting me as it always does, Anil's phone lay there on the side table, clearly forgotten in a momentary lapse. I could hear the pattering of the water from the shower. I stood next to the nightstand, staring at his phone, paralyzed. I knew exactly what was in store, and yet, I tried to stay optimistic.

Don't do it. You'll only regret it. Maybe this time you won't be right. What if it's true? You believe him, don't you? Trust is important. He said never again. You actually don't have a right to violate his privacy. What if he treated you this way?

I wish my inner voice wasn't so strong. I wish my gut wasn't always *so right*.

Suddenly, the water stopped, and I realized that I didn't have long to take action. Anil was humming his favourite song, and it was clear that he was in an exceptional mood. Did I really want to risk ruining a perfect Sunday morning? I could already hear him saying, *just drop it. No heavy talk today*. But I couldn't help myself.

I reached for his phone, my hands trembling. Meanwhile, on the other side of the room, I heard rattling of the vanity drawers and then the buzzing of his electric razor, which meant I had more time than I thought. I held the phone in my hands, sat at the edge of the bed, and stared at the locked screen. I wondered why he would think to lock his phone if he had nothing to hide.

As luck would have it, I managed to unlock Anil's phone just as he was finishing his shave. I quickly scrolled through the text messages, and then, I found her.

I had heard her name before. Anil had casually mentioned her in conversations, and she had a knack for showing up at parties unexpectedly. I always felt that her gaze followed him wherever he went, lingering longer than it should. I often noted that she was always the last to leave, and it was clear to me that she had mastered the art of teasing. Anil said I was imagining things. That she was in a happy relationship and had zero intention of leaving her man. Besides, he reassured, he only had eyes for me. I was the prettier, the smarter, the thinner and the better one. Why would he ever risk losing me? And just like that, I told myself that I was clearly delusional. I should know better than that and besides, he would be insane to cheat on me.

I closed my eyes, took a deep breath and looked down at his phone.

Hi babe. I miss you. Can't wait to see you.

Me too. I want you so bad. I can't wait to hold you, lick you, caress you and make sweet love to you.

The door was opening, so I quickly placed his phone back on the side table. Anil walked out of the bathroom looking as handsome as ever with his glistening skin, wet hair, freshly shaven face, mischievous eyes, and playful smile. In a momentary lapse, I became lost in this image. An image that I had held in tenderness for so long. An image that I had made more sacrifices for than I care to admit. My heart swelled up and I felt myself losing control.

The bittersweet moment quickly melted into an ugly, messy tantrum. I burst into tears, blurting out *how could you* as many times as I could humanely manage while hyperventilating and making sounds, I didn't know I was capable of. First, I was humiliated, and then I felt pain. The deep, seething pain awoke a core wound that I didn't even know existed.

I'm not worth it. It's true. He just proved it. And so have other men. How many times do I have to fall to learn?

This was not the first time I had been in an unfaithful relationship and the reason that I have come up with as to why it kept happening to me is that I believed I couldn't do any better. It's because I was scared of ending up alone. It's because I couldn't imagine anyone else loving me as much as he did. It's because I knew the good memories would haunt me and cause so much pain. I felt it was a risk to expose someone new to my imperfections and my flaws. I didn't want to risk learning to love all over again. I'd take the cheating, and lies in stride, forgive, and stay.

I didn't believe that I deserved any better.

FIRESIDE CHAT

I met Dimple through another book project and had the pleasure of seeing her speak to a crowd about shame. I watched the crowd as much as I watched Dimple and I was profoundly impacted by how she shared her story of shame and how it led her somewhere better. I have come to adore this woman for the honesty she shares when she speaks about things that many people prefer to keep hidden.

People go through some negative experi-

ences but eventually some people are able to look at that experience and pull some things from it that they are grateful for, even though the experience has been difficult. Are you able to pull things from your experience that you are grateful for and if so, what are they?

I believe teachers come in all forms. The obvious ones are my parents, educators, and my children. The not so obvious ones are the men in my life who caused me serious emotional pain. The teachings that came from my negative experiences are like gold and I am so grateful for the lessons I have learned.

I learned so much about mental illness and now, I truly appreciate the complexity of it. Leading with empathy and compassion is key and I now relate to others who are struggling.

It took me a long time to recognize, but I learned that I wasn't doing anything wrong to deserve any of it, and that the problem wasn't with me.

I learned the importance of boundary setting. In my most destructive relationship, I did not set any boundaries and that allowed for the continuous cycle of destruction.

I am grateful for the ability to forgive and love Anil. People often wonder why I don't hate him. My answer to that is that hate only hurts the hater. I would much rather offer up love because it is the highest form of devotion.

When I reflect on all of the things I have learned, I realize how much I've grown as a result of the pain I experienced, and do not doubt that because of this, I can now be a better partner to the man I am with today. It was hard for me to recognize these lessons during the messiness, but I now know that pain serves a purpose, and for that, I am grateful.

When you were facing the most difficult point in your journey, what was the best decision you made and why?

The day I walked into my therapist's office to ask for help was the day my life changed, for the better. Unfortunately, there is still a stigma around mental health and going to therapy. Often it is seen as a sign that something must be wrong with a person, or that they are *broken*.

When the time finally came for me to feel fed up with the constant betrayal, I knew I was in some deep water, and no matter how hard I tried, I was entrenched in its toxicity. I was desperately looking for a way out, but did not know what to do. I did not want to talk to my friends about my situation because I knew that in their eyes, the easy solution was to leave Anil.

One thing that I have learned is that unpacking a complex situation like mine requires professional help, whether that be in the form of a coach, a counsellor, or a healer. Counselling and coaching made a world of difference in my life and both forms of therapy are my go to's when I'm faced with life's challenges.

If you were deprived of all but one of your coping mechanisms, which one would you keep and why?

Journaling feels like one of the best ways for me to connect to my intuition, and during times of high stress, journaling and moving my pen is what keeps me sane. To me, writing is medicine. Writing connects me to my voice and to others. When I look back to when I was married to Dev, during times of extreme conflict, I turned to writing. Instead of verbally expressing myself to my husband, and risking another heated argument, I would write letters to him. I cannot recall a moment when Dev rejected any of my letters, and in fact, he told me how much he appreciated them. It softened him.

My last relationship, the one with Anil, was quite different. In fact, I went through a bit of a traumatic experience related to my journal. He went searching for my journal in my home unbeknownst to me and I learnt that he had taken photos of many of the pages from my journal. I felt ripped apart, and violated. After that, it took me a while to return to my journaling practice. There was a lot of fear around feeling safe to write truthfully. That period of my life was very difficult. Besides being a soft cushion to fall on, journaling allows me to release, reflect and breathe a sigh of relief when I need it most.

What would you do differently if you were to find yourself experiencing this "event" again as your much wiser self?

One of the things that I would do differently is I would set healthy boundaries and commit to them. Setting boundaries was something I learned about *after* I had been through a couple of toxic relationships. On paper, setting boundaries makes so much sense but I have only recently begun to implement them in my relationships. Without boundaries, I was acting out in unhealthy ways. I would push back in resentment and anger during times of conflict. I became a nag, which basically just led to further disconnect in the relationship. I lost respect for myself and felt my self worth wither away because even though I hated what the relationship had become, I stayed and kept repeating past patterns.

I also had to learn the difference between setting boundaries and setting up walls. I was really good at setting up walls with the men in my life, which meant giving them ultimatums but never following up with the consequences. I would withdraw, ignore and engage in passive aggressive behaviours. None of these tactics worked and instead, just made me angry, which was not good for my mental or physical health.

If I had set healthy boundaries, my exits from toxic relationships would have been much quicker. Boundaries are like my north star. They help guide me and make decisions and keep me true to myself.

When you were in the darkest point in this experience, do you recall your thoughts and feelings? Can you share them with us?

I certainly do. It was a combination of anxiety and fear. Anxiety has a way of becoming all-consuming and I think the driver behind it is fear.

I would constantly question my negative experiences with men. Why was I always in this situation of infidelity and how did I attract it into my life. The worry of *"is he cheating on me?"* riddled my days. These thoughts did not allow me to be fully present in my life and I'm sure I missed out on a lot during those years.

I had never known what it was like to feel safe and secure in a relationship and now that I do, I am shocked at how much I deprived myself back then. I am not kidding when I say that my nervous system was on 24/7. There was a perpetual underlying layer of fear all of the time.

In order to curb and control the uncomfortable feeling of fear and anxiety, I would constantly be on the lookout for solutions to fix the relationship. It was as if I didn't want to let my guard down because if I did, it would mean that I'd have to accept that the relationship was over. I'd be on the hunt for a coach, then a counsellor, then a couples' retreat, and the list was endless. All of that just to salvage the relationship. I was desperately chasing something that couldn't be caught and I felt like I was on a never-ending hamster wheel.

It was exhausting and depleting. Not only had I lost my self-worth, but I was running myself to the ground. It was just a matter of time before I'd realize that, physically and mentally, I wasn't able to carry on. It took self-destruction for me to take myself seriously.

What was the "pivot point" in this experience where things began to change for you in terms of how you thought and felt about your situation? How did your thoughts and feelings change and how did that change impact the outcome?

There finally came a time when it clicked for me that "real love" wasn't supposed to feel this way. When I looked back at my life, I realize that the depth of the work that I was being called to do was not as simple as it looked. In fact, it took an entire team of people to help me put the pieces of my life story together. My team consisted of a naturopath, therapist, friends, family, healers, and myself.

A pivotal moment for me was when I finally left my last toxic relationship which was with Anil. It was in January 2016 when I walked into a new therapist's office and made my claim. I said to her, "I'm here to see you because I need support to leave a toxic relationship that I haven't managed to let go of." It was huge that I was clear about what I wanted, and that I outright asked for help. My therapist helped me set up strong boundaries and guided me through the process especially during times when I didn't trust myself enough to pull through.

What are the top three lessons you have learned from this experience and how do they impact how you live now?

TRUST THE PROCESS: I was gifted some tough life lessons, and by trusting the process, I trusted that a beautiful ending was just around the corner from the messy middle. It was hard to trust when I was in the middle of a crisis, but without my belief, I would not have been able to propel myself forward and likely would have remained paralyzed and consumed by fear. I also learned the importance of investing in a team to support me because I could not do the messy work alone.

Self compassion = Self Love: What I am learning is that true Self Love has to include acts of Self Compassion. Part of the reason I stayed in my last relationship for so long was out of compassion for Anil and his compromised mental health. In the process, I risked my own health. Where's the sense in that? Through therapy, I learned to show myself compassion, and put myself first so that I could detach from a harmful relationship.

Raise your Vibration: I needed a healthy amount of time alone before I jumped into another relationship. For me, it was well worth the wait and the work. I needed this time to shed my old life, to renew and to raise my positive vibration. When I was able to raise my positive vibration, I could attract the love I deserved.

How has intuition served you on your jour-

ney? We often discount the intelligence that our " gut feeling" has - how has it served you?

When it comes to making difficult decisions, I rely on my intuition to guide me especially when I am feeling lost. My intuition has never failed me, and in fact, whenever I ignored my intuition, I was led astray. In all of my experiences with infidelity where the men cheated on me, my gut was always right even before I had concrete proof. However, because I did not have "proof", I often neglected my inner voice and convinced myself that I was being paranoid. When I would eventually find out about the affairs, my first response would usually be relief followed by sadness and anger. I felt relief because I knew I was not imagining things, that I had been right all along, and because I was moving in the right direction. That gave me some peace in the midst of chaos.

Instead of resolutions, I pick words for the year to emphasize my focus. This year, I've chosen the word SPIRIT as my Word for 2019 because I know how powerful intuition is and I want to do whatever I can to further connect with it so that I can strengthen it.

This year I am engaging in practices that will lead me to SPIRT, which includes my higher self, and my intuition. Meditation is now part of my Morning Rituals, and I practice it daily. I am also exploring oracle and tarot cards because they are a playful way for me to tap into my own intuition. When I harness the energy of the moon, plant medicine and crystals, I feel vibrationally aligned with my higher self. I engage in weekly voice lessons because singing gives me goose bumps and I believe that goose bumps are short cuts to intuition. And I'm leading each and every day with my core desired feelings which are Rooted, Peace, High Vibes, Spacious and Radiance (Danielle LaPorte, *The Desire Map*). When I connect with these every morning, my day unfolds divinely.

MEET DIMPLE

Dimple Mukherjee is an Occupational Therapist, Women's Coach, Speaker and Contributing Author. A Graduate of Queen's University, Dimple combines more than twenty years of experience helping women harness the healing and transformative power of self-care rituals and female connections for personal growth.

Personal photograph

Dimple is the creator of Bindi Parlour, an in-home facilitated gathering for women to embrace themselves and to create positive shifts in their lives through meaningful conversations, journaling, storytelling, and more.

Dimple is the author of a *Morning Rituals E-Guide* and regularly hosts a **10-Day Morning Rituals Challenge**, to help others harness their inner wisdom. The *Morning Rituals E-Guide* is available for FREE on Dimple's website: www.dimplemukherjee.com, and her chapter, "So. About that affair: When shame translates into self-destruction, the only way out is through connection and self compassion" can be found in the collection *Women Rising (Vol. 3)* on Amazon.

Dimple lives in Toronto, Ontario, with her three sons.

7

DYING IN MY PRESENCE

JENN KERR GASPAR

"Be open to shifting your beliefs. It will not serve you to remain stuck in a state of suffering."

JENN'S STORY

My dad's presence was larger than life. He was an avid cyclist, and took great pride in keeping active and physically fit. He ate from the outside isles of the grocery store and enjoyed vibrant discussions over the latest innovations and social paradigms. He valued education, receiving degrees from several Universities. He became a nationally recognized artist after his retirement from the clergy. He was my mentor and hero.

Eighteen months after he was diagnosed with a rare, terminal illness, my dad died. I had the privilege of walking with him through the last phase of life.

This journey for me began one summer morning in 2016. My dad biked over and appeared at my back gate. I was on a ladder taking photos of a bird's nest in my apple tree. I told him to come over and take a peek at the baby robins. The nest was in a hollow on the trunk and just above his eye level. He held the trunk, lifted his head and pretended to see. As I hopped off the ladder, I watched as he rocked back on his heels, braced his arm on the tree to support his weight and attempted to pull himself onto his toes. I realized he couldn't do it. I was unprepared for the journey that followed.

At first, dad was treated for Parkinson's disease. His mind was sharp, but his posture and facial expressions became rigid. When diagnosed early, many people can find great relief from medication and exercise that slow the progress of the disease. Dad's symptoms however, were getting rapidly worse. Odd new symptoms were appearing faster than doctors could diagnose them. To me, it seemed like he had been misdiagnosed.

I began a journal so I could document his health. I had everything on file so when I accompanied Dad at medical appointments I could advocate for him with concrete facts. I kept track of dates, blood pressures, dosages of medications, times of meds, number of falls, and photos. It was fact-based and I took comfort in feeling as if I could be in control of something. It was perhaps a way of processing grief. In hindsight I'm glad I did it. This was with my dad's permission and support. He hoped my notes could one day help someone else going through a similar terminal illness.

The final diagnoses for my dad was Multiple System Atrophy or MSA. MSA is a rare (one in 100 000) and fatal neurological degenerative disease. It progresses rapidly and there is no cure. It attacks the autonomic functions of the body such as: blood pressure, sweating, swallowing, temperature regulation, talking, digestion, elimination, speaking, moving. It attacks without mercy, yet his mind remained intact. He did not suffer from dementia. There is no remission. There is no recovery. The average age of onset is midlife. Seven years or less, from the initial appearance of symptoms, is median life expectancy.

I became an expert on the disease. I immersed myself in medical journals, reached out to world-renowned experts in the field, and became a fierce advocate for those living with Parkinson's and MSA. Knowledge empowers.

We kept him at home as long as we could. I accompanied dad to a geriatric team assessment and the decision was made to hire home care aids to come to the house to assist with bathing Dad. The house was assessed and we implemented all recommendations including the installation of a chair lift, an exterior wheelchair ramp, extra rails in each room, and multiple assisted mobility devices.

Eventually, for both dad's safety and to minimize the strain on the rest of the family, we all reluctantly agreed, that is was time to put Dad's name on a waiting list for a room in long-term care.

In late February of 2017, he had a serious fall and lost consciousness. The paramedics came and took him to the ER. That was the last day he ever walked. He stayed in hospital for about three weeks until he was stable enough to be moved to a long-term care home. I remember biting the inside of my cheek so I wouldn't cry in front of him. He dealt with the losses heroically.

This transition to the care home was one of the most difficult times for me emotionally. I felt powerless. I helped decorate Dad's room. I curled up with him on his bed and we watched *The Godfather*. My mom, my brother, and I would rotate spending time with him. As his illness progressed, I knew it would be his last summer. We rented a van for the month of July so Dad could come to the family home for a meal and nap in his beloved yard. He savoured these moments and was extremely appreciative.

By August, I had to come to terms with my own limitations. I was recovering from jaw surgery, dealing with a flood, and doing my best to juggle single parenting my beloved daughter and son, while caring for a dying parent. The stress took a toll on me physically and I found myself on bedrest with Shingles.

Before long it was Christmas. December 25th was the last day Dad came home for a visit. It was a brutally cold day to bundle up for travel, but he was willing. He died in January 2018 after a heroic battle with Multiple System Atrophy. I had the honour of being a small part of that battle.

FIRESIDE CHAT

Total transparency, I teach with Jenn and because I have been the sole caregiver of a child who has a chronic illness, I could see what other might not see when Jenn showed up for work everyday. Caregiver burnout. Emotional detachment (emotion is a luxury one cannot afford to have if you are carrying it all.) I was curious about her insights into this experience and invited her to share her wisdom with us.

If you were deprived of all but one of your coping mechanisms, which one would you keep and why?

For me, acquiring knowledge was a monumental coping mechanism. Researching Dad's illness helped me feel anchored, when the progression of his deteriorating health was surreal. I found that I could handle the stress better when I kept my mind occupied. I put aside my emotions and become analytical.

There were times when it would be late, my kids would be asleep, and my house was quiet, yet my mind was not. Typically, these were also times when new stages of Dad's illness appeared, which were new losses to process and new limitations to adapt to.

Frequently I would begin these nights trying to meditate, but I could not quiet my inner dialogue. I would journal, but still feel restless, so I had to try something new. These were the times I would immerse myself in research. I needed to learn how the disease progressed. I needed to learn what other caregivers found useful. The process of acquiring knew knowledge about a topic I knew literally nothing about, was liberating, and empowering.

I could not control how long my dad had left. I could not control which of his autonomic systems would cease to function. I could, however, control how much I educated myself about Multiple System Atrophy. I felt at least if I could help myself understand the disease I would not be nurturing any false hopes. I began to prepare myself for the symptoms Dad was likely to face as he neared death.

On those restless nights, after digging into some research, I could relax, meditate and get to sleep. It seemed to become a routine for me whenever new circumstances arose. It was definitely a way to process my emotions without becoming overwhelmed.

Interestingly, this is still how I continue to cope with unexpected challenging events. Gaining wisdom will never be something I will regret.

What role has letting go, surrendering, forgiveness, fear or limiting belief systems played in how much you suffered/succeeded?

I think once I accepted that I could not change what my dad was going through, a certain serenity and wisdom emerged. I was no longer preoccupied when with Dad.

For the first couple of months after Dad moved into long-term care, I was in attack mode. Everyone took the brunt of my anger. I lashed out at doctors, nurses, the care home aids and staff supervisors. I felt like I knew what my dad wanted, and needed, better than any anyone. In reality though, nothing was black and white. There were unreal expectations placed on all parties.

At the time, I didn't see all the care that my dad was receiving. I felt like I was somehow easing my dad's suffering, by micromanaging his care. I was in fact causing him undo stress and I had to back away and trust the professionals. It was hard to let go. I felt protective. I could understand my dad, but by this point, many of the staff were unaware of what he was saying. He could no longer dial the phone. He was frequently unable to reach his call button. It broke my heart.

There came a point where I had to surrender and stop complaining and realized that it was not beneficial.

I had to soften my tone and apologize. It is quite humbling when you have to go and explain a text that you accidentally sent to the senior staff supervisor of your dad's care home that was meant for someone else. Mortified at my carelessness, I even called my cell provider, hoping I could somehow call back the text, because it had not been 'read' yet. I hoped I could magically make it disappear, especially given the late hour it would be time stamped. The technician just laughed. Yep. That was a lesson on surrendering too.

Our meeting ended with a hug, tears, and forgiveness. We had a good laugh too and saw each other as human. In hindsight, it was the best possible thing that could have happened. Perhaps it was divine intervention.

I really began to get to know the staff. I saw how kind and hard-working many were. I got to know them as human beings. They got to know me, not as an angry daughter, but as an advocate for long term care home needs.

This experience has also taught me I sometimes have unrealistic expectations of myself and it has been healthy to turn forgiveness inward. I used to think that was somehow a cop-out, but instead, I know now that it is liberating.

I want my belief system to continue to evolve. Always remember that we need to adapt to new experiences and knowledge. Be open to shifting your beliefs. It will not serve you to remain stuck in a state of suffering.

What is your advice to people who are struggling with the same experience you have lived through?

Know that this too will pass. There will be a time when you will look back on your current struggle with a different, broader perspective. It doesn't feel that way in the moment, but it's the truth. We are remarkably resilient beings and we move through and forward. Be gentle on yourself.

Call on others. Accept help from others. Support will arrive in your life exactly when need it, and sometimes it will be from unlikely sources.

Consider writing a letter to your loved one. I felt compelled to share private thoughts with my dad that I do not think I could have expressed in a conversation. I wrote my dad a series of letters. Write to them as though it is the last time you will have opportunity to communicate. You might chose never to give the letter to anyone, but just the process of writing these thoughts is therapeutic and comforting.

Practice being in the present moment with your loved one. This is that space in between memories and thought. Let yourself be present with your loved one. This can be as simple as the act of washing your loved one's face.

Cherish the difficult times. Many do not get to experience this kind of life transition with a loved one.

Grief is not something you experience only when a loved one dies. You feel grief when you are experiencing any profound loss. It could be a marriage breakdown, retirement, or a child moving away. I found holidays and family celebrations more difficult for a time. Know that it is okay not to be okay. You will process grief on your own time, in your own way.

There is a strength within you that will appear. Call on it. It's a quiet, background essence that will serve when you are ready. You will know what I mean. It is unmistakable.

What was the "pivot point" in this experience where things began to change for you in terms of how you thought and felt about your situation? How did your thoughts and feelings change and how did that change impact the outcome?

I felt a loss of control when Dad had to be

moved from our family home into long term care. In some ways, I felt guilty as though I was abandoning the man that had given so much of his life to support me. Logically, I knew it was the only solution given the staff and equipment required for his needs. I was grieving his move when there came an end to my sense of defeat and hopelessness.

I had a Eureka moment when I visited him one day at his care home. He had been eating chocolate cookies and had chocolate all over his hands and face. He was unable to maneuver his arms to reach under a running tap. He had always taken pride in maintaining a tidy, well-groomed appearance.

I had him by the sink in his room. It was a simple, beautiful moment. I filled a bowl with warm water and soap. I had washed his hands countless times before, but I had a shift in awareness on this particular day. I sat beside him and gently put his hands, one at a time, in the water. Methodically and gently washing each finger with the washcloth, I was taken by the connection in that moment. He was so appreciative.

It became an act of love. I saw the situation differently. I would consciously cherish these times. I felt like I wasn't fighting anymore. I accepted that he was dying from a terminal illness. I stopped obsessing about the disease and what it had taken from him.

Embracing this stage of his life allowed me to change my mindset. I made a conscious effort to be in the present moment when I was with him. At first, I had to remind myself of the colours and the sounds around me, but as I practiced, it became second nature to be completely present.

I found washing his face therapeutic. I was moved by his grace as he surrendered to these moments. There was no other agenda. It sounds peculiar, but this pivot point allowed me to experience the remarkable process of dying. I could embrace the present moments rather than focus on the past. I was free to feel my grief.

What is the top lesson you have learned from this experience and how does it affect how you live now, and what advice would you give to others who may have gone through something similar?

This experience taught me to take care of my ter-

rain. By terrain, I mean my whole self; body, mind, and spirit.

Your body will kick into 'flight or fight' adrenaline-mode to help you cope with an extremely intense life event. That stress needs to be released because your body will keep hanging on to it. This fact is so important when dealing with a prolonged stressful situation. Do whatever you need to do to dissipate that tension. It will keep accumulating in your body and inevitably, your health will fail.

There was a stretch of time where I was doing acupuncture twice a week. I found yoga and binaural beat music effective. I made constant use of a journal. Writing emotional days' events was a way to release feelings that were no longer serving me. My journal carried part of that stress for me.

Mediation and prayer became daily rituals. Doing something you enjoy that taps into your creative side is another form of meditation too. You can draw, paint, photograph, dance. Don't be concerned about productivity or a finished product. That's not the purpose, though it may end up being an unexpected bonus.

Even if it is the middle of winter, spend at least five minutes walking outside every day. Fresh air and daylight will help. I really try to do some form of physical exercise daily. Gardening, walking, biking, push ups, intense house cleaning; anything that works up a sweat. This is magical for your hormonal system. I cannot state enough how important it is to get physical activity.

Limit your consumption of media, especially the news. Upsetting stories will increase stress in the body, sometimes without your being aware of it.

Feed your body real food. You will be shocked at how much better you can response to challenges with clean fuel.. Simply put, over the long run, I crap out if I eat crap.

Know that you are never alone in those darkest of times. Talk about it in a form that works for you. Consider joining a local support group, or perhaps an on-line forum. Share with your extended family, friends, colleagues what you're going through. Supportive people will appear if you call on them. Many will come forward that now are in a position to give back. You will build new connections too.

With practice, I have come to know my symptoms when I am not coping. I know if I have not been maintaining my terrain. If I let things slide, I do not beat myself up about it, I just get back into what I know works for me.

How has intuition served you on your journey? We often discount the intelligence that our " gut feeling" has - how has it served you?

It is rare to witness death. Had I not listened to my intuition, I would have not been at my Dad's side when he died. Death, like birth, is sacred. It is an event that cannot be put into words. It is an experience I will never forget, and I will humbly cherish the fact that I was given the opportunity to be present with my Dad.

It was a cold Friday in January. I was on my last day of sick leave for jaw surgery and would be returning to my class the coming Monday. I felt compelled to get to my Dad. There was a sense of urgency and intuitively I knew. The feeling was unmistakable, though hard to describe. It was a pulling sensation as though I was being drawn to my car.

I was singing to a playlist I made for my dad, as

I drove across town. The music spontaneously stopped mid song. The pulling sensation between my navel and sternum was now so strong. Words that were not my own came to me. *Be in the silence*. An overwhelmingly calm essence directed me. I drove on.

My body felt like it was synchronized with a presence I could not see. Time slowed and everything was sharp, and intensified. Every minute was vivid and I was in the moment. No mental chatter distracted me.

After parking at his care home, I went to lock my car. The key simply would not work. As I entered the lodge, my phone vibrated a text notification. Instinctively I glanced to read it, no text.

My senses felt heightened in the elevator. I could hear every mechanical sound. It was like high definition vision. All of the colours were vibrant. The doors closed, then opened again. No one was there. The elevator doors flinched, for lack of a better word, several times. I waited in silence. Thoughtless. I felt a draw, almost like a magnetic pull through my upper stomach. It was a profound, unmistakable feeling.

The lights flickered as I ascended to Dad's floor.

My phone buzzed again from my pocket. This time as I took it out, it wouldn't unlock. The screen froze. Battery fully charged.

The pulling feeling felt tangible, magnetic, tactile and I thought it would be somehow visible to everyone. I knew. He had waited. I held his hand and told him I loved him and that it was okay to let go. I felt love everywhere. There was no fear. I kissed his forehead and just sat in his presence.

I would have been filled with regret if I had not listened to my intuition. The wisdom I gained in the experience are without limit.

MEET JENN

Jenn Kerr Gaspar is a teacher, artist, writer, public speaker, and mother. Her charisma, candour, and compassionate nature, draw her audiences in to her personal experiences. She is a natural storyteller with a wry sense of humour. She considers herself an ever-evolving, creative optimist.

Her teaching career spans over two decades. She continues to build a strong rapport with students, families, and colleagues. She builds connections with people from all ages and backgrounds.

She had her first art exhibition in 2006. Her paintings are inspired by narrative moments and her thought-provoking portraits have an impressionist style.

Personal photograph

Awakened by a near-death experience, Jenn began an intensive spiritual journey of self-discovery. She is a fierce advocate for the vulnerable, and also supports humane treatment of animals and stewardship toward the environment.

Jenn loves spending time with her two children. She also enjoys gardening with her yellow lab Kennedy. She enjoys biking, nature hikes, skiing, and pretty much anything else that gets her in motion.

She creates in her home studio and resides in Saskatoon, Saskatchewan, Canada. More information is available at: www.jennkerrgaspar.ca, facebook.com/jennkerrgaspar.

8

LAYERS OF LOVE

BEAUTY H. FAULKNER & LERAE S. FAULKNER

"Even in the darkest of times, your soul light shines."

LeRae's Story

I was fifteen years old when an illness called Guillain Barré Syndrome (GBS) tore apart the life I knew and sent me on a life-changing journey I wasn't prepared for. GBS is a neurological disorder where the body's immune system attacks the peripheral nervous system leading to paralysis. I was so young, and due to the severity, my case was considered rare.

The illness coursed through my body so rapidly

that I became paralyzed from the neck down and was put on a ventilator within 24 hours. Through my journey I experienced unimaginable suffering and uplifting triumphs.

My mom and I decided to write our story in a book called *Love Strength Faith*. I chose to write my part of the story in a diary format, as a terrified, fearful fifteen-year-old girl, unsure of what was happening and with no way to communicate with the outside world. Many memories from my experience on the ventilator are fragmented into pieces, or snapshots in time that I only have a brief recollection of. What I do remember vividly, is the fall, and my descent into GBS. Here is an excerpt from our book *Love Strength Faith*, moments before I was put on the ventilator:

October 20, 2006

My body is shutting down faster than anyone anticipated. I have no control over what's happening to me. I've always needed to be in control, which makes this experience my worst nightmare. I'm becoming more frightened. I'm trying to calm myself down by not thinking about what's going on inside my body. I'm beginning to gain control over my thoughts. Yes, it's helping me calm down.

The room I'm in is spacious and quiet. There are two sliding doors in front of me through which I can see into the reception area. I'm propped up on my hospital bed, which is how I can see what's happening around me. What's weird is I'm unable to fully open my eyes, and, even if I could, my vision is blurry. Suddenly, I feel short of breath. There's a nurse with me. I tell her I'm having trouble breathing, and she left. She freaking left!

I'm gasping for air, and it feels like I'm suffocating. I try to call for help, except no one's around to hear me. Where is everyone? I feel like the nurse is never coming back, and I'm going to die. I don't know why I can't breathe. Are my lungs failing? My fear of the unknown overwhelms me. I'm not ready to leave. My life is just beginning. I'm only fifteen! Oh my god, I can't breathe. No matter how hard I try or how desperately I gasp, there's no air coming into me. Finally, three nurses come back into the room with a doctor, but they're moving so slow! They know I can hardly breathe—why are they still moving so slow? I just want them to hurry. I'm dying—don't they know I'm dying here? My fear is turning into rage. They're taking too long. I'm going to die if they don't move faster. I try asking for help one last time… (Page 4)

Beauty's Story

It was mid-afternoon in 1998, and I was laying on my bed contemplating ending my life. I yelled out loud, "God, please there must be another way out of this pain than ending my life. Please show me what that is, my children need me."

This heart felt plea led me into a deep dive into the shadow-land of myself and into the world of energy medicine where I was introduced to the concept that everything is energy. After studying and practicing the healing arts for ten years, this concept transcended into a knowing, and became a guiding force in my life.

On October 19th, 2006, I was shown through a life-changing event that I was actually *one* with this guiding force, and that everything was connected, and nothing was ever out of place. This was the day when my beloved daughter LeRae became paralyzed from the neck down and was placed on a ventilator. Guillain Barré Syndrome (GBS) was taking over her body. The moment she was ventilated the world I had known vanished into the abyss and I was catapulted into a new world, where I was shown all things are possible, miracles exist, and everything is energy. This was the beginning of many mystical magical miracles and the start of my own soul awakening experience. This profound knowing shifted me out of a grieving mother and into LeRae's Master Healer. Even though my heart was shattered and filled with grief, I chose to focus on her healing and stay in the light. I remember consciously pushing my feelings and emotions to the back of my mind, since I knew processing them at that time would serve no one, especially LeRae as she was literally fighting for her life. I also knew, through my own self-healing journey, if those emotions surfaced it would be exactly when they were meant to, and it would be my time to heal.

The moment I chose to shift into LeRae's Master Healer, everything aligned. Healers from near and far began to pray for her or visit her in the hospital when they were called to. Family, friends and healthcare workers who were destined to help save LeRae's life also showed up in divine order. I experienced a magnitude of mystical, magical miracles, witnessed spontaneous healings, and felt a love so benevolent, there are still no words to describe it, even though I have tried. I witnessed this love hold LeRae as she moved through pneumonia, double pneumonia, a serious leg infection, numerous bladder infections, multiple fevers, and choking episodes while she was ventilated. Her heart rate would fluctuate which led to many episodes of tachycardia, where at one point the doctors needed to stop and restart her heart. Through all of this turmoil she was still healing at an incredibly fast pace, leaving many of the medical staff in disbelief and in awe of the progress she was making. Thankfully, LeRae made a miraculous recovery and my life has forever changed. More about our remarkable story can be found in a book LeRae and I wrote together called *Love Strength Faith*.

FIRESIDE CHAT

Synchronicity brought Beauty and I together in

life a few times, although each meeting was fleeting. It is only by looking back at how this all unfolds that it seems somewhat magical, otherwise, it seems ordinary. Through Beauty I met LeRae and learned of their story when I attended their book launch. I had fought a health battle with my daughter and I wondered where they had found their strength for healing. At the launch, I sat there biting my lip trying not to cry because I knew the agony and the fear they shared all too well. I was still praying to step fully into my own miracle with my girl. I also knew that if I asked questions of them, I would get different answers than someone else may share given Beauty's background. I didn't really know LeRae, but I adored her by the end of the launch.

What do you believe have been the key factors to you successfully coming through this experience to possess some wisdom that you share with others who may be facing the same type of challenge?

LeRae

I believe the key factors in my ability to rise above my illness and defy the odds were my determination, tenacity, will to live and my trust in others. I said yes to every prayer, healing modality, helping hand, and medical intervention. I welcomed everything and everyone who was willing to help and pray for me. Allowing these people into my life offered me support and love I could never have imagined. When I came off the ventilator and I was able to breathe again, a feeling of indescribable peace washed over me, and even though I was still in a tremendous amount of pain, I felt like I was living in a state of peace and tranquility. I was so grateful to be alive! To breathe, to love, to live. I was determined to do whatever it took to walk and dance again, to appreciate and be grateful for everything in my life and know that whatever I set my mind to I can accomplish. I believe there is a hidden strength within all of us, and when we need it, we can tap into it and change the course of our lives. Sometimes we can do it on our own, and our strength is enough, other times we need the strength of others to help us rise.

Beauty

Some of the key factors that helped me through this profound life-altering experience were my beliefs. I had just spent ten years of my life committed to a dedicated practice of becoming 100% responsible for my own energy, being conscious of my own thoughts, feelings and beliefs and witnessing the power of love in action as a force of healing. The moment LeRae became ill, I knew as her mother I was going to do everything humanly and energetically possible to help save her, and I knew I had the tools to do so. What I didn't know was that I would need to completely surrender my will to divine will, meaning, I would need to hold on and let her go at the same time. This was when I realized that most of what I had been practicing was still more of a concept in my thinking mind than a feeling in my body. I thought I had experienced the highest vibration or feeling of love that was possible after giving birth to my two children. I also thought I had mastered the art of managing my own energy and the power of my thoughts. After watching LeRae rise and fall repeatedly in PICU and witnessing the rest of my beloved family and friends move through this unimaginable miraculous experience, everything changed for me. I can still remember the moment when I was praying to God to have mercy on LeRae's Soul and the profound feeling of love that was pouring out of me from my shattered heart like a tidal wave, that began to fill with an indescribable benevolent energy; a life force so powerful and immaculate it felt like a miracle was about to happen. In that moment, I fully understood. The love pouring out of me was the same love that created me, that created all life.

"Oh my God" I cried. "I am loved this much, LeRae is loved this much, we are all loved this much!" And you, beloved reader, are also loved this much.

WHAT WAS the worst advice people gave you or the most annoying things that people said to you when you were in the deepest point in suffering?

LeRae

There were moments when I was on the ventilator when the doctors and nurses would say things out loud, possibly thinking I couldn't hear them, or not recognizing that my cognitive function was still there.

I could hear.

I could think.

It was my body that wasn't responding to my thoughts. My emotions were in full force and hearing some of the things the medical staff said didn't help the situation.

Just before I was about to be ventilated, I overheard one of the doctors say, "If she makes it, she will never walk again." Before my Mom could say anything, I remember turning my head and asking her, "Is that true, will I never walk again?"

She pressed her face up against mine and said, "No, none of what he said is true, I love you, and you will make it through this."

There were many other moments while I was on the ventilator when I overheard the doctors talking, which seemed to become a running theme, because all of them would forget that I could still hear them even though I was paralyzed. I would hear comments like "She still can't breathe on her own," "Her chance of a recovery is minimal," "No more pain medication" even though I was still in excruciating pain.

There is one more comment that stands out, and it is somewhat unbelievable. I was experiencing a high fever and my mom and a nurse were trying to break my fever by placing icepacks around my whole body. It wasn't working. My body temperature was melting the icepacks faster than they could cool my body down. Suddenly, the nurse leaned down and whispered directly in my ear: "We are trying to bring your fever down, if your fever doesn't break soon, you will have brain damage."

I know she meant well and was trying to help me understand the severity of the situation but hearing that as a young girl, having no control over what was happening to my body, could have sent me into an all-out panic, making my fever worse. The next thing I knew my mom had the nurse out in the hallway, and a few moments later, the nurse came back to my bedside, leaned down and whispered: "You can do this, you can bring your own fever down, the ice packs are working."

Words are powerful. It is important to think before you say something, especially when someone is in a life or death situation.

Beauty

One of the most heart-breaking things to hear was, "She needs another test," especially, a nerve conduction test called an electromyogram. This test determines the amount of severity or damage within the muscles and nerves of the body. It was absolutely essential in the beginning of LeRae's illness to have this test completed, so the doctors could diagnose what stage of nerve damage she was experiencing. It was determined that she was in the 4th stage, meaning, the myelin sheath surrounding the nerves from her knees down was completely destroyed. This was why the doctors wanted to keep testing her to see if their findings would improve after she received treatment.

I remember the moment Ed and I decided that we were no longer going to allow this test to be done. LeRae was in PICU, on the ventilator and being examined by another neurologist. He decided he wanted to do another nerve conduction test and asked the nurse to bring the machine in. The moment he turned the machine on, LeRae's face winced in pain, which meant she was feeling every shock. Ed and I looked at each other in horror and said "Stop, no more testing!"

The doctor tried to convince us that these tests were necessary and absolutely needed in order to monitor her for nerve activity. Ed, who is a soft-spoken person, loudly stated, "No you don't!" And that was the end of the nerve conduction tests.

What was the "pivot point" in this experience where things began to change for you in terms of how you thought and felt about your situation? How did your thoughts and feelings change and how did that change impact the outcome?

LeRae

The moment I came off the ventilator, I made a choice. I made the choice to live. I was determined to prove the doctors wrong and take those first steps. The road to a full recovery was going to be long and rocky, yet I knew I could do it. Life was on my side, and I was ready to take full advantage of it. Before I could even think about taking my first step, I knew I needed to retrain my body and teach myself how to do everything all over again. My brain had to learn how to communicate with my nervous system and I needed to rebuild my body from scratch because all my muscles had atrophied. I am thankful I made the decision to work for it, and truly dedicate myself to my health and recovery. If I hadn't made that decision or if I had listened to what those doctors said and let those thoughts lead my recovery, I wouldn't be where I am today.

Beauty

One of my pivot points manifested in the examining room at St. Paul's Hospital. I was sitting on a chair directly across from LeRae when she started choking. The Doctor who was examining her called for the nurse and she quickly placed a bowl under her chin so she could spit out the extra saliva. I watched in disbelief as LeRae's body rapidly shut down in front of me. Her body became more limp with each second that passed and she could no longer control the muscles in her eyes. This memory is making me cry.

There was a feeling of complete terror and helplessness that filled my body, along with an inferno of unbridled rage boiling up inside me. My mind was racing with terrifying thoughts all about the possibility that I was about to watch my beloved daughter die, and there was nothing I could do to stop it. As I watched this terrifying event play out, LeRae began choking uncontrollably. Oh, my God, her throat is closing, this is it, she is going to die, she is going to die right here in front of me. Why, why, why, please God no! Then came the loudest whisper I've ever heard in my life: *close your eyes, close your eyes, plant your feet, plant your feet.* So, I closed my eyes and that's when everything changed. My thoughts and feelings shifted from terror and rage to a profound feeling of peace and indescribable love. It was the beginning of what I call, a Mystical Magical Miracle.

It was also the moment I moved away from the grief, hopelessness and the fear as her Mother, into her destined Master Healer. This was when I knew all the spiritual self-healing tools I had been practicing and integrating within myself for the past ten years were being called forth to help save her life.

What are the top three lessons you have learned from this experience and how do they impact how you live now?

LeRae

What will be, will be.

For me, this statement means to trust. To trust

in myself, the universe, and however life unfolds. Having faith in something greater than myself has helped me be at peace with how life unfolds. To take life as it comes and instead of reacting out of fear, I try to accept that there is a reason and meet every situation with love and an open mind. This is something I tend to forget, as I am human, and my emotions often rule my life. When this happens for me, I remember what will be, will be, and it helps to calm my mind and settle my heart.

I am making a difference just by being here, by being me.

Years after my life changing experience, I began to doubt myself, to doubt my greatness, my strength and my life. I wanted to find my purpose, my calling. I came through this near-death experience and I felt I should be doing more. I should be putting myself out there, helping people, telling people my story and sharing with the world what I had accomplished. I expressed this to my Mom, and she told me that I was making a difference just by being here, by being me. This changed the way I was thinking and allowed me to return to the grace and gratitude that I have for living.

Slow down, have patience, and live in grace.

Before GBS, I lived at a very fast pace. My mind and movements were always moving at lightning speed. I walked, moved and lived fast, almost to a point where I was missing my life. My experience with GBS helped me find patience, presence and a slower pace within my world. I often live in the future and slowing down, having patience and living in grace, brings me back to the present moment and allows me to find peace. I am reminded to slow my thoughts down, take a few deep breaths and come back into my body.

Beauty

Honestly, as I ponder this question, I can only think of one lesson or teaching that has continued to flow in and through my life, blessing upon blessing, since October 19th, 2006. It was the day when LeRae, my son Austin, my husband Ed, my family, friends, healers and caregivers showed me that the truth in the concept, "We are all One" was no longer a concept. A new world opened within me and I was shown that all things are possible, miracles are real, and everything is energy. It also showed me that

Love is an unstoppable force, Strength is immeasurable, and Faith is the conduit from which Grace arises. LeRae's own unique soul journey reminded me of my own journey and why I call myself Beauty. It reminded me to see the beauty in all things, bless everything and everyone with love and be grateful for every breath I take: To honor and cherish myself as much as I honor and cherish the people in my life: To live in the moment, practice what I teach and live my life in joy, with the wonder of a child and to creatively express myself through the light in my eyes, the love in my heart and the song in my soul.

And, when the darkness comes and my fear voice becomes louder than my soul voice, I remember, I was born soul first, human second and I have nothing to fear. I have learned when I face my fear and take a deep dive into the shadow land within myself, golden nuggets of truth and precious gifts are revealed. If your fear voice has become the only voice you hear, or you feel lost and alone, please ask for help. We are all in this together.

How has intuition served you on your journey? We often discount the intelligence that

our "gut feeling" has - how has it served you?

LeRae

When the GBS took over, my intuition went into overdrive and shifted my soul-self into a higher state, where I was able to communicate with my mom telepathically. My intuition/soul-self began leading the way, doing all it could to help me survive, bringing in healers, healthcare workers and people who would pray for me every day. My intuition saved my life because I became one with it, there was no separation. As I recovered and regained my strength the intensity of my intuition lessened, I no longer needed it at that magnitude anymore. As the years have gone by, I realize I have stopped listening to my intuition as often as I used to. I believe I am just starting to tap into it again and allowing it to guide me as I move through my life.

Beauty

I remember what that 'gut feeling' felt like when I was a little girl, and as I grew older, how it became much more refined, and by the time I was in my late twenty's I was definitely making better choices for myself. The same gut feeling that was guiding me up until that point, changed dramatically after my 33rd birthday. I began experiencing a painful, tingling sensation in my right foot which ultimately moved into my left foot, and eventually up both my legs creating a chronic pain condition. After many months of uncertainty and unexplained pain, I found myself moving through a spiritual awakening as I contemplated ending my life. It was shortly after that point in my journey when all *the Clair's* woke up, meaning all my Clairsenses (Clairaudient, Clairsentience and Clairvoyance) were front and center. This was when I found myself in the middle of a cosmic circus and the receiver of an overwhelming amount of intuitive information. Thankfully, this new level of awareness led me to a twenty-first century Shaman, Reiki Master and numerous healers who were able to help me navigate all the crazy, exciting, and sometimes scary moments I was experiencing. For the next ten years I practiced, studied and learned everything I could about the healing arts and how to manage *the Clairs*. Eventually, I was able to teach myself how to turn them off, like a light switch, so I could live my life more peacefully and within my own sovereignty. Then, Guillain Barré showed up, attacking LeRae's body from the inside out. In a moment of complete terror, I was shown through a profound vision that it was time to turn *the Clair* light switch back on, so I did! I was instantly transported into what appeared to be another layer of intuition and everything I knew to be true before that moment disappeared. New teachings and levels of awareness emerged from within me and I was able to champion LeRae in the fight for her life and help her live. So, in a nutshell, my intuition has literally become a life saver with the words *Thy Will Be Done* always echoing in the background.

MEET BEAUTY

Photo Credit: LeRae Faulker

Beauty H. Faulkner was born and raised in

Saskatoon, Saskatchewan. In 1997, her soul-awakening journey began, leading her to self-realization through deep study and devoted practice of alternative and energy medicine. She is passionate about the soul's evolution and helping others elevate their lives. She is a singer, song writer, recording artist, the founder of Beauty's Rainbow Productions and the co-author of *Love Strength Faith*.

MEET LERAE

LeRae Faulkner was born and raised in Saskatoon, Saskatchewan. After overcoming a life-threatening illness, she began travelling the world, expressing her creativity and living life to the fullest. She also attended the college of Saskatchewan Polytechnic, graduating with honours and a diploma in therapeutic recreation. She has a passion for helping others, which motivated her to share her story as the co-author of *Love Strength Faith*.

To learn more about Beauty and LeRae, and to purchase *Love Strength Faith* please visit www.-heartsoulanthology.ca. You can also find *Love Strength Faith* at McNally Robinson Booksellers, Indigo, Soul Food Grocer, VitaJuwel Canada,

Crystal Cove and Twig & Squirrels Wild Goods, all located in Saskatoon, Saskatchewan. Their book is also available online on Amazon.ca and IUnivsere.com as an Ebook.

Contact: lsf@heartsoulanthology.ca

Backcover Photo Credit: Molly Schikosky

Photo Credit: Tammy Zdunich

9

IT'S ALL IN YOUR MIND

LOIS A UNGER

"When I no longer believed that overeating would save my life, and I fully trusted in myself, the real change started."

LOIS' STORY

Had I just eaten all of that? I looked around and saw empty wrappers strewn about the floor and seats of my '82, red, two-door hatchback. The first stop was at a convenience store for something sweet; butter tarts, chocolate cupcakes, coconut sno balls, danishes, chocolate bars, and pastries. I opened the wrappers as I walked out of the store, and I gulped down a few by the time I open the car door. A few minutes later, and I was at my next stop: the drive-thru up the street. I hid the wrappers from the convenience store snacks in the bag because I did not want the next cashier to see I was getting more food. This time I got real food after my sugar fix. I ordered a couple of burgers, pies, and a shake, and a lot of ketchup. I couldn't eat it fast enough. I was in a trance. I was alone, and at that moment, felt great. I was blissfully happy and listened and sang along to my music as I drove. Food and I got along. We loved each other.

As I got closer to my house, I realized I forgot to discard the wrappers. Will these all fit in the brown paper bag I got at the drive-thru, I wondered. I had to get rid of them so no one would know. I had just cleaned out the car last week. Usually, no one else was in my car, but just in case. This will be the last time, I promised myself.

It was getting harder to get in and out of the car. I had to get a special seatbelt extension made, as the car factory belt no longer fit around my body. By the time I got home, I just wanted to sleep. With so much food to digest, my body was tired and lethargic. I couldn't think clearly, didn't want to talk to anyone or do anything but lie down and left alone.

I would often tell myself tomorrow will be different. I will start - again. Tomorrow will be the perfect "start day". But then I would convince myself that I couldn't start because it was my cousin's birthday, or friend's anniversary, or full moon. I wanted my start day to be mine, just mine. I had these same thoughts repeatedly for a long time.

The days filled many years of lonely moments. Black polyester pull-on pants, and loose shirts became my uniform. I never wore dresses as hose were hard to put on. I also wore men's sandals. Some items from the women's department just didn't fit.

I was facing pain, hurt, and despair, and food had a tight grip on me. From the outside, I looked overweight, but I appeared to be normal. No one knew the disaster that was within me. I was drowning. I felt disconnected from my truth, purpose and core values. What are they? Who am I? I experienced symptoms of brain fog, mood swings from sugar highs, and depression. Some days I prayed just to sleep and die. I used to feel alone, even in a crowd. I thought that I didn't matter, and was worthless because I was overweight.

After one particular celebration, there were many trays of home baking leftover. The kind I just loved. Easy to eat, soft and creamy, cut up in two bites or less. I sat on the floor in my tiny house, on a 70's flair style rug with red and brown swirls. Stacks of sinful goodies surrounded me; butter tarts, brownies, peanut butter marshmallow, Nanaimo bars, chocolate chip bars, coconut squares, and many others. I was in sugar heaven. I decided to try them all- again and then again. Instead of packaging them up and freezing them for later, the compulsion to eat everything overtook me.

One day, as I was spinning out of control, I finally came to a stop. I looked around, listened, and suddenly knew it was time to make a change. I felt relieved and full of fear at the same time.

I started learning about visualization, positive I

am statements, to slow down, to listen to inner self- care needs, eliminate worry and practice daily mindfulness. My lifestyle and body size started to change just by the way I was thinking. As I experimented with various new thought patterns, I truly enjoyed my life more. My physical self changed, but more importantly, so did my mindset. The changes only happened after I started practicing mindful living in a healthy and natural way. There were no magic formulas, no invasive actions. It was just me. I did it on my own, for me.

As everyone is different, it was important to seek out a personalized plan to create my best self. Following a food and fitness plan has resulted in a reduction of over 150 pounds and over 55 inches. My shoe size is even down, and my rings are too big. I donated 95 bags of my clothes to Goodwill. My non-scale wins are even more impressive. I have more energy, sleep soundly, am making better social connections, and every day is a wonder. It has been over five years, and I have kept the weight off, and my healthy lifestyle keeps getting better. As time passes, the numbers become less significant.

I believe that I am the sole creator of my life, and that is incredibly empowering. I am so grateful every day for the giving universe. When I started believing and trusting in myself, endless opportunities came my way. This is my story, and it is what has worked for me.

FIRESIDE CHAT

I met Lois when she took one of my courses and became intrigued with how she had changed her life so drastically, and I admired her aspirations to live big each day forward. It was as though the lid had just come off her box and she realized the possibilities that lay ahead of her, and she had this swirling, energetic excitement about where she was headed. Let's dig in and find out more about her how!

When you were facing the most difficult point in your journey, what was the best decision you made and why?

It seems as though, for most of my life, I have lived in two different worlds, but in one body. The physical self, which was my heavier self and the other, was the dreamer future self. I lived in the future a lot. Even when I was in a fury of empty wrappers from chocolate bars and fast food, I still had a glimmer of hope that I would not overeat forever. I wanted to change and stop being a slave to sugar-laden, unhealthy foods. The best decision I made was to never stop believing in myself.

I kept many secrets in that future vision of myself. Part of me believed I could actually pursue the passions I was longing for, but something kept holding me back. With my larger body size, and thoughts only surrounding food, there was no energy to access. When I take on projects, I like to give it my all, but when I was in a foggy state from a binge, I knew that I was nowhere close to achieving that. When I was overweight, I felt stuck in the present and took things day by day. During my weight reduction, I started thinking about the future, and my passions. Could I really pursue any of them? Am I good enough? I realized that I now had options. I always did, but now food was not in the way. The questions kept coming, and the universe kept delivering.

No matter what my body size has been, I have

always kept a vision of what and who I want to be and did not push life away. I listened to my inner voice, and the payoff has been rich.

What would you do differently if you were to find yourself experiencing this "event" again as your much wiser self?

If I ever go through this experience again, the difference would be that I know I need to take action to make a change. I love to read and conduct research about things that interest me. When I was at my low point, the more I researched the next magic formula for weight reduction, the more overwhelmed I felt, which would then lead me to binge. It was a vicious circle for many years. I still love research, but now, I follow through on my action plan, instead of feeling overwhelmed. I food prep, plan meals and, prepare for enjoyable body movement. When I travel, whether it is across the city or miles on a plane, I do not rely on airports, airplanes, or gas stations to have what food I will need. It has become a habit to take care of myself in that way and feels great. Creating my own recipes and choosing which foods are best feels empowering. Being mindful sets me up for success. When my brain receives the proper nutrients, the decisions I have to make become easy.

What was the worst advice people gave you or the most annoying things that people said to you when you were in the deepest point of suffering? Explain.

Some of the most annoying, and insensitive things that people said to me during my deepest suffering were:

- *You have such a pretty face.*

- *Why don't you just have one?*

- *Just have a little - for me.*

- *Why can't you just stop eating sugar?*

- *You have such hidden talent.*

- *Not so much.*

- *Don't be so loud.*

- *One bite won't kill you.*

- *I would want you all the time.*

- *Quit eating.*

After my weight reduction, I was asked many questions like:

- *How did you do it?*
- *How long did it take you?*
- *How many pounds in how many weeks?*
- *You're not going to lose anymore? Are you?*
- *What exactly did you eat and when?*
- *Did you exercise? How much? Which ones? When?*
- *Why now?*

No one was concerned about how I actually felt. How ironic! Sadly, when I was overweight, neither did I. Food replaced my feelings, and I often asked those same questions of myself.

If you had advice for your younger self, what would it be? Could this advice help you sidestep some suffering? If so, how?

The advice I would give to my younger self is believe and trust in yourself. I would remind myself that life is short and only gets shorter. I would want to tell myself to stop and think about how my destructive eating behavior is affecting my life and my health.

What I know now is food is like insurance. If you eat nutritious, healthy foods, the outcome will be worth it. Binging and overeating place our bodies into extreme stress, as does lack of body movement. Digestion comes to a halt. It is a vicious cycle.

When I was binging, my thought process got derailed. Instead of feeling and living, I was eating. I missed a lot because I was so worried about where the food was, where I would sit, how much I would have, and who would see me. I was so focused on food that I did not get to enjoy my surroundings or the people in my life. I have learned to slow down and focus on myself. With a clear mind, I get to decide what is right for me. I think living in the moment is when you truly make the best memories. I would tell my younger self to focus on the present day, and that it is ok not to know everything.

Some other advice I would like to tell myself is to learn and change as you go. Learn to read your body and own it. Quit self- attacking and empower yourself with divine guidance. Be the person you want to be now. Internal dialogue carries a particular frequency, and with the right positive response, you can create a healthy, vibrant and life that is full of energy. Connect with your higher self. It will unite you with love, success, abundance, and happiness.

What are the top three lessons you have learned from this experience and how do they impact how you live now?

Through my own discoveries and studies, *I learned that people's relationship with food represents how we approach life's greatest challenges.*

When I finally knocked at the door of curiosity, and the door opened, miracles started to occur. *I learned that having the right mindset could bring me freedom from food.* I sought out information, studied holistic health and wellness, meditation, and learned to achieve my desired end results from the beginning. Being mindful and grateful on a daily basis inspires me to take risks and go after my dreams. I live in the moment and do what I love.

I learned how to build a foundation of self-care, connect to a higher power, and tap into my intuition that I had previously buried. My brain now has new thought patterns. I learned that taking care of myself is not selfish. I am a better person for it. When you ask and believe, be ready to receive.

How has intuition served you on your journey? We often discount the intelligence of our "gut feeling". How has it served you?

The farther you fall, the higher you will rise. I fell right through the bottom and crashed. Trying so long to hide my overeating, one day I decided to see what this new door had opened for me. Could this be real? Did I really have a hope of a new life? Was my brain fooling me? Many questions came at me, along with doubt and insecurity. I knew I had the knowledge to make health a priority. I had done a lot of research and experimenting. Now it was time to implement the plan. Something within me spoke, and this time, I listened.

The heart is the body's central system. It runs the show. Ego is in the brain, but the ego might misinterpret certain messages. This is when to pay attention to your higher self and listen for direction. This is when you forge ahead and leave others' opinions behind. A vivid vision brought me to a new understanding. I plunged in, feet first, and moved towards joy and fulfillment.

Day by day, I transformed into a different person both physically and mentally. As time went on, I started to feel more confident moving my body. I stopped needing the seatbelt extension, I chose healthy food, and overeating was no longer enjoyable. I smiled more, I interacted more with friends, and I was just simply happier. I could deal with stress or obstacles in a more efficient way. When I no longer believed that overeating would save my life, and I fully trusted in myself, the real change started.

What was the "pivot point" in this experience where things began to change for you in terms of how you thought and felt about your situation? How did your thoughts and feelings change and how did that change impact the outcome?

After starting and stopping many diets and spending a lot of money, I was finally at a standstill. Considered morbidly obese by the charts, I felt frozen, yet, something deep inside me whispered that I would not remain this way forever. I had already missed so much of my life because my entire focus was on my weight and body size.

I have always liked reading self- help books, and about positive psychology, but suddenly, I started to apply what I was reading to my life. This was definitely a pivot point in my experience. From my reading, I was able to confirm that I needed to follow my heart, and I became aware of why my previous way of thinking had not brought me lasting results. I persevered and practiced, read and studied about my newfound skill, which ironically, had nothing to do with how I approached food. I could be eating something healthy, but if I had negative thoughts while doing so, it would not digest properly. I could actually gain weight from negative thinking. I learned that if I could give my body love and gratitude, I would notice small shifts. Suddenly, I felt like I was on a new route. I loved waking up in the morning, taking walks, seeing the color of flowers and trees and getting to know the new me. For so long I had no idea who I was or what I liked. My brain waves were suddenly lit up, and I knew there was no going back. The new destination seemed challenging, exciting and I was ready to explore. My heart finally felt like it had a home and I was right where I belonged.

MEET LOIS

Lois enjoys writing and photography. She loves to explore lines and photos between learning about food, fitness, travel, positive health and the holistic body. She is often singing and dancing to her extensive music collection while creating in the kitchen and crafting a new recipe. When she is not hunched at the keyboard, she can be found exploring in nature, reading true crime, at the gym, research data on articles for magazines, volunteering, or dreaming about the next getaway to somewhere. Born a prairie girl, and Saskatoon is home now, she is excited to become a brand ambassador in skincare, fashion, fitness, food, and self-care for women over age 50.

She has studied in mind-body connection, yoga, meditation, nutrition, and competed in two marathons. Currently working on her own book about her lifestyle transformation, she is also

IT'S ALL IN YOUR MIND 195

planning to speak and share about her experience and how she became fabuLOIS.

- Website: www.loisunger.com
- Email: fabulois.05@outlook.com
- Facebook: @FabuLois

Photo Credit: Lois A. Unger

Backcover Photo Credit: Lois A. Unger

10

LOSING MY GRIP

JENNIFER SPARKS

"It is a fragile space between hope and despair, and you tread carefully."

JENNIFER'S STORY

In 2011, I was celebrating turning 40 and had made some big plans for the year. I took an educational leave from my job as a teacher to complete postgraduate studies, and luckily, for me, I was doing it all through an online program. This meant I had considerable freedom to get my studies done from virtually anywhere in the world. And that was my plan. Study. Travel. Celebrate life. Shake things up a bit. Grow and stretch.

At that time, I had been divorced for about six years. My son was 13 and my daughter was 12. Both were responsible kids, so I felt that I could easily slip away to feed my soul in some other ways because, as many of you likely know, being a single parent is a full-time job. This was going to be the year for *me*.

My year on leave started with a trip to Santa Monica in November with my sister and mom on my birthday weekend. It was interrupted with a distressing call from my ex-husband that my daughter had an episode of concerning behaviour where she zoned out and didn't respond to anyone for a short period of time.

When I returned home, I took her to the family doctor and described what had happened. He agreed that this needed further investigation. A few weeks later at her parent-teacher conferences, I was informed that my daughter was becoming defiant, sleeping at her desk, acting confused, and was not listening to instructions. This report of her behaviour was odd because she had always been a good, respectful student.

Things continued to deteriorate over the next month until the morning of December 31, the magnitude of what we were walking into became glaringly apparent.

I had just hopped in the shower but was pulled back out when I heard frantic hollering that something was wrong with my daughter.

My friend had placed my daughter in the recovery position but she was not breathing, her eyes rolled back in her head, and her arms and hands curled into her chest.

Time. Stood. Still.

I grabbed the phone and called 911 while I prayed. I honestly thought we were too late.

She regained consciousness but floated in and out, unable to speak or communicate. It took about an hour before she knew who I was. She had apparently had a seizure. We were sent home from the hospital later that night but I had this feeling in my gut that brought me great anxiety.

The following week it happened again. Two weeks later, again. Also, in between these episodes, she acted really of out of it, distracted and not herself at all. We were on the waiting list to see a neurologist, but our frequent ER visit bumped us up in the priority list.

Soon, we entered the world of tests and doctor appointments as I prayed again that this would be something we could deal with and there would be some way to bring her health back around quickly. She had been a healthy, active kid, so I had a million things running rampant in my mind. In January, my daughter was diagnosed with Epilepsy, and we were hurled into a new world of seizures and chaos.

Just as I was hoping to take a year to celebrate my beautiful life and travel, I became homebound with my girl trying to navigate a foreign world of seizures, memory loss, anxiety, depression, insomnia, medications, injuries, hospital visits and fear like I had never known. I was hopeful that we would quickly stabilize her on medications, but that did not happen as I had hoped.

Flash forward five years, and imagine a thousand nightmares in between and we were still fighting to gain control over her seizures and some predictability in our lives.

We were wounded and battle weary.

Everything about our lives had changed. I was suffering from caregiver burnout but had no idea how to shift things. We had developed a medically co-dependent relationship. I was anxious when I left her alone. My sleep had been interrupted so many times from seizure alarms or choking sounds that I didn't even know how to sleep anymore. I often found myself waking up while running down the hallway because I thought I heard something or needed to check to make sure she took her meds. If I called out to check on her and she didn't answer, or I heard a plate hit the ground, or saw her school's phone number on my phone, I received an immediate hit of adrenalin that took hours to recover from and my body was in a constant state of stress.

I was with her as much as I could be because I felt like if I was there, I could keep her safe. I pulled her off horses, theatre stages, and out of cars to prevent her from aspirating while she was seizing. I caught her mid-step, held her on chairs so she wouldn't fall, or got the icepack when she did. I cradled her head above the bath water so she wouldn't drown. I found her in the backyard face down in her blood after she seized and smashed her face, found her sitting in strange places uncertain of where she was, and I pulled hot curling irons off her face.

I tried to help her maintain emotional stability, but I could barely keep myself together as the fatigue continued to thicken. The medications caused behavioural changes that made our house a war zone. There was conflict between us, which changed how I parented because I felt unsafe in my own home. There were 911 calls for seizures and safety concerns because sometimes I was afraid for my wellbeing as her brain raged on medications, altered and confused. I lost my little girl to an invisible monster that could shape-shift when I wasn't paying attention. I was living with a stranger that I felt entirely responsible for keeping safe, but honestly, we were sinking.

As her primary caregiver, I detached emotionally because thinking about the individual pieces of loss over the years was too overwhelming. I lost my freedom, and she, her teen years. I lost my daughter and mourned who she had been and as I became a robot caregiver who had to conserve energy to manage the lives and emotional wellbeing of two people. My son was often left to figure things out on his own because I was dealing with my daughter's health issues. I was losing my grip, and it felt like caring for her was killing me. It had been five years of the same thing, and regardless of how I tried to adjust our sails to catch the wind, little was changing.

Just when I thought things couldn't get worse, they did. She went status (a state of constant seizing without recovery in between seizures) and ended up in trauma. I was terrified of how all this would end for us. Many times, I called back my prayers to end this suffering, because I didn't want to be misunderstood by the "universe" and have her taken away from me for good. I was often afraid of my thoughts.

While this was the lowest point, it was also a place where everything shifted. ER docs brought in a new neurologist, we got a medication change, and when we left the hospital that time, she became stable for the first time in five years. She has now been seizure free for two and a half years, except when we have adjusted her meds.

Innocently, I thought to reach this goal would bring peace. It has not been that way. While it has been better, there remains a constant battle with mental health issues, severe anxiety, depression, memory loss, and confusion. We still deal with the medication side effects and mental health challenges daily.

What her stability has offered me is time to reflect on the role of the caregiver when supporting someone with a chronic, longterm illness. Especially, how vital the wellbeing of the caregiver is to keeping both people afloat. Looking back, I realize I made many mistakes, and they have had a substantial impact on the last eight years of my life. Today, as I reflect on my experience caring for my daughter, I am almost amazed we both made it this far, but I remain somewhat anxious for the uncertainty of what the future looks like for us.

FIRESIDE CHAT

What are the key factors that allowed you to come through your experience, and what wisdom could you share with others who may be facing the same type of challenge?

I put many of the difficulties my daughter and I

faced into little boxes and learned to stay in the moment. Planning was difficult because one neurological blimp could change everything I had planned. It was incredibly frustrating and a waste of time and energy. I had to learn to go with the flow and to take one thing at a time, being okay with letting things go when I had to. Hanging on to plans, or refusing to let go of my disappointment made me miserable. For example, I struggled when I had to miss work. Being my daughter's primary caregiver meant that if she went down, she needed me. Some mornings I would be on my way out the door to work, and something would happen by surprised, and then it was suddenly impossible to leave the house. I became okay with dropping some of the balls in my life. As someone who cares deeply about doing a good job at everything I do, I had to come to terms with prioritizing what was most important and then taking anything extra in stride. Yes, that meant I took time off from work, and I said no to invites from friends and family, but it was because I had no option.

My priorities shifted, and I spent more time and energy focused on the things that mattered, at this moment. Sure, I wanted to be a great teacher, sister, and friend, but more than anything, I wanted to be a good mother and help my girl. I did not want her to feel alone or like a burden so when I was with her, I tried to be 100 percent with her. Once I had re-prioritized things in alignment with my values, I had much less disappointment and was able to deal with the crises as they arrived.

I also had to learn very quickly not to take things personally. When holding her well-being in my hands, I was the sounding board and the verbal punching bag for emotions she was struggling to process as a 12-17-year-old with a chronic illness. The medication she was taking changed her mental functioning and caused her great frustration. Some days she would blast me with it, but it was never about me doing things wrong or messing up. It was more the fact that I was the one who there. If I took things personally, I would have been destroyed.

If you were deprived of all but one of your coping mechanisms, which one would you keep and why?

The winner for this one is Gratitude. I never actually practiced gratitude until I was in a very dark place and struggling to see any hope at all for a fulfilling and purposeful life for either of us. I gave gratitude a whirl because I was out of options and I felt a shift immediately in how I perceived our situation. I had become so focused on all the negative aspects (seizures, medication side effects, worry about "what if", hospital stays, injuries, school work, mental health), that I stopped seeing the good (supportive friends and family, supportive employers, the sun on my face, a solid night's sleep, access to health care, deep breathing). Once I started consciously identifying the good, I saw more of it. What we focus on expands, and I had been focusing on the negative, so when I switched my focus to the good, I felt so much better and I was much more capable of dealing with the curve balls that continued to come our way.

I am now at the point where if something happens, I react with gratitude, instead of catastrophizing what took place. The other thing that has shifted is that I often notice when particular events blocked me or us from experiencing something worse. One day we were in the mountains hiking and she wanted to climb a steep shale rock and I immediately felt like it was a bad idea. I would not let her go alone, even though she had been stable for some time. I surveyed the terrain, and thought if she goes down, all of these "bad" things could happen. I went with her and stayed close. We got down safely and into the car. Moments later she had a seizure. Having the seizure was awful, but having it in the safety of the vehicle and not on the mountainside was a blessing. Cultivating a response of gratitude has changed everything about my perception of our circumstance.

What would you do differently if you were to find yourself experiencing this "event" again as your much wiser self?

I think part of me denied that this would be a long-term challenge for my family. I kept saying I could manage for two more weeks, and then two more, and two more, and never did anything to get solid supports in place. We limped along from week to week, patchworking a schedule with people to watch her or provide support, but nothing was set in stone. This resulted in lots of unknowns surrounding more unknowns. Chaos.

Looking back, I would have figured out a way to

get sustainable support in place so that the weight wasn't all on my shoulders most of the time. Initially, I could manage, but over the long term, the pressure became too much. So denying the possibility of what I was facing didn't serve me well. I never let myself imagine the negative outcomes because I always felt like if I thought it, I might bring it. What was neglected right off the bat was my self-care. I was beaten down slowly until I wasn't much use to anyone anymore and was mentally and emotionally exhausted. I am still dealing with this exhaustion as I slowly let it rise in doses I can address.

Secondly, I would have attended a support group meeting and reached out to people in the Epilepsy community sooner. When you show up in a room full of people who "get it" without you having to explain all the little details, there is enormous relief that you are not alone. Plus, they provide stories of hope and a treasure chest of coping mechanisms and resources. I know that resource is there, even if I am not currently using it.

Finally, some professional insight into the struggles of the caregiver would have been beneficial.

I remember sitting in ER one night as we dealt with another crisis. I moved into autopilot and was going through the motions doing everything to make sure she was safe, and her needs were met. She stopped me and asked me if I was upset because I was emotionless and detached. It was then that I realized emotion was a luxury that I couldn't afford at the time, on top of all the other things I had to take care of on a daily basis. I shut everything off to make it through each day and then put things into their boxes so I could make it through the night. I felt horrible for denying my daughter access to my emotions because it did remove some of the compassion from her care, but many times, it was too overwhelming to begin processing my feelings just in case the damn broke. There was so much held in there waiting for a time it could be processed, and I knew if that damn broke, it was going to be messy.

What role has letting go, surrendering, forgiveness, fear or limiting belief systems played in how much you suffered/succeeded?

Let's just say that when you let go of things you have no control over, you put some stuff down. Things get lighter. But, it is not always easy. I had been wrestling daily with keeping my daughter on her feet and trying to control everything around her (most of it was wasted energy because it changed nothing). I would worry a lot about the "what if's", but then I realized that if I could worry her back to health, I would. But I can't, so this worry about the unknown is wasted energy that is better spent somewhere else.

I started focusing on what I could control like medication compliance, support for adequate sleep, buffers for when she had a virus and was more likely to seize, and I learned first aid so I could do my very best in any situation. I put the rest down. I surrendered it all and the hardest one of them was to realize that if she had a seizure and I was not there to catch her fall or to help, it wasn't because I was a shitty mother. It just wasn't humanly possible to be there all the time for another human being. I had to forgive myself for any time I felt like I "should have" done something differently. How the hell did I know? I was doing this blind.

I do feel entirely convinced that letting go, surrendering, and forgiveness has played a significant role in my recalibration as a caregiver. We do the best with what we have in any given moment. Period.

What was the "pivot point" in this experience where things began to change for you in terms of how you thought and felt about your situation? How did your thoughts and feelings change and how did that change impact the outcome?

Our pivot point was the evening she went into status. It was the day all the wheels came off. It was the all-time low and I struggled. I did not understand what was happening, what had triggered her, or what the outcome was going to be. However, in this crisis, various new medical personnel came in to support her, and from then on, things started to shift. All of a sudden, we had new eyes, a new approach, new meds, and a new outcome.

After struggling for over five years, we were standing on the edge of finally having seizure control. I began to have a new sense of hope. I started to imagine bigger and better things for her again. Every day that passed that she was seizure-free, my fear lessened a little bit. It is a fragile space between hope and despair, and you tread carefully. Every day I checked the box on the calendar and as I continued to flip the pages over weeks passed with seizure control and then months and I can't even believe that we are now over two years controlled.

There is so much truth in the saying that sometimes the breakdown leads to the breakthrough because we had to look at things differently. Desperation makes you open to new ideas. While I would NEVER want to see my daughter in that type of situation again, if she didn't hit rock bottom, we very well may have continued as we had for the previous five years barely holding it together.

Seizure control meant she had more freedom, and so did I. It meant she could start learning to drive. It meant we could remove the seizure bracelet, bed alarms, and allow for unsupervised showers. It meant space. Deep breaths and expansion. New experiences, catching up, less supervision, and more letting go.

It meant untangling our weird co-dependent relationship with a tremendous amount of patience and humour.

What are the top three lessons you have

learned from this experience and how do they impact how you live now?

People want to help but do not know how to help. Get clear on what you might need.

I have so many awesome friends and I could have called any one of them for help, but I didn't. Not because I didn't need it, but because I couldn't even articulate what I needed and if I couldn't articulate it how would they know what I needed? I also had some shame and embarrassment around what state my home was in when we ended up at the hospital. Seizures are not pretty and cleaning up after them was something I felt I needed to do myself to maintain privacy. I also felt guilty about not being able to handle it on my own. Furthermore, I was often moving from moment to moment, so there was not much preplanning in my life. I wish I had the mental space to formulate a few things that friends could help me with when we ended up out of commission.

- A go-to grocery list or a few meals that I knew my kids would eat.
- A cleaner to hire – please arrange it and let her in.

- Pet instructions – written out and easily emailed or texted along with my door code.
- Someone to sit with her for a couple of hours while I came home to shower and take a nap because she had extreme anxiety in the hospital and hated being left alone.
- Someone to sit with her while I walked the dog and cleared my head because I never had downtime.

Be a caregiver, but also care for yourself.

When you are a caregiver, you are often tending to the needs of another and their needs demand attention now, not later. It is easy to slip into the abyss and forget all about your own needs. Your eating habits tank, the lack of sleep creates stress on your hormones; you don't even have time to go for a walk or to clear your head or to sit in a coffee shop and stare at the wall. You crave not being needed just for a second. Above all, prioritize your well-being because when you start to hit the skids, the person who is depending on you is likely to go with you. At that point, you have two people in crisis, not one.

Limit the fallout and arrange to take care of yourself. When I was depleted, we suffered more than we needed.

Understand this is their fight, but you can provide support.

I learned this after expending all of my energy trying to move a depressed person out of bed. JUST GET UP! JUST GO TO SCHOOL! She wanted to, but literally could not, and no amount of begging would change anything. Instead of screaming at a brick wall, I changed tactics and asked her what she needed. I tried to offer distractions. It was not about my agenda anymore, but hers. Let's go for a walk and get outside. Let's go for a drive and see sunlight if you are too tired to walk. Let's get a tea and sit by the river. No amount of my urging could speed up how she was able to participate in life. I just had to let go of some expectations, and when I did, everything was easier.

How has intuition served you on your journey? We often discount the intelligence that our " gut feeling" has - how has it served you?

I have heard that your intuition is the strongest

in the areas of your life that mean the most to you. If this is true, then it is not surprising that my gut guided me a great deal in my caregiving journey.

There were many times when my daughter was in an altered state mentally because of medications and her behavior was not acceptable to me. I would be rolling up my sleeves to prepare to address the issue, but my previous ways of parenting were silenced by what felt like a guiding arm being placed across my chest in anticipation of a car crash. I felt halted. So I changed my approach. I observed more and allowed for time and space between a situation and how I dealt with it. I could sense the energetic shifts in her. Dark days felt very different than lighter ones.

When I stepped back and observed, I would often notice that there was something neurological taking place. For example, I would look at my daughter and notice she did not look like herself, or her eyes held something different in them, or her body seemed tense and ready to explode.

When I listened to my intuition, I managed to

navigate these situations with her very differently than I would have had I jumped in and reacted to whatever had taken place.

There were times, where my emotions were amped up or I was moving through the day sleep deprived or afraid, and I seemed to lack the capacity to allow for the time and space that was needed. I would react, which would then escalate the tension. I heard my gut, but my emotional reaction took over. In one of these instances I ended up with 56 stitches in my arm, in another, I ended up locking us both into the house deadbolts and all, restraining her, and calling 911 for help. Maybe it didn't need to come to that, but I had missed or ignored all the intuitive cues. I had been guided, but I did not listen.

Further, much of what I agreed to or didn't agree to in terms of her medical care came from my gut feeling. In what instance would I call 911? When I could feel my gut screaming at me that something was not right or different and sometimes I couldn't even articulate what my gut knew, but I knew we needed medical support.

It was never wrong. Many of my "hunches" about her triggers have come from my gut feelings, which led to further investigation. Usually, these feelings were so strong I could not possibly walk away from them. They nagged me until I either acted on them, and was proven correct, or ignored them, and wished I had not done so.

To feel my way through the hardest parts and relying on my intuition to guide me has proven to provide the most successful outcomes.

MEET JENNIFER

Jennifer Sparks is an author, speaker and life strategist at www.jennifersparks.ca. She has spent almost fifteen years exploring the science of happiness and mindset. Fascinated by how people can change their lives by changing their minds and then their behaviours, she coaches privately and speaks across Canada about happiness, motivation, gratitude, and mindset.

Her bestselling books *WTF to OMG, Happy on Purpose, The Gratitude Transformation Journal* and *The LIFEMAP Infinity Planner: Life, Dream and Business Planning System* can be found on Amazon. Her upcoming book, *50 Shades of Happy: How to Master Your Thinking and Dominate Your Day* will be available for pre-order on Amazon shortly and launches in the summer of 2019.

AFTERWORD

I learned many years ago how sharing your story can heal your heart and soul. I also learned that when you release your words into the wild, you have no idea where they will land and whose lifeline they may become.

Story is magical.

Story is part of all of us.

Story is what binds us together.

Story can be what keeps us afloat.

The women who have been brave enough to share about their transformations and triumphs have all come into my life in various ways and, no doubt, for a reason. While imagining what I wanted this project to look like, these women were brought across my path and to my attention because they were sharing parts of their story and I was intrigued to learn more. They were also all different, yet I could see the common threads.

It wasn't always the details of the story I wanted to know more about. I wanted to know how they managed to make it to where they now stand and how they felt about the challenges they had been through.

Did it make sense now that they could look backwards into their lives?

What did they learn?

What can they pass along to others to help them?

Did they become different humans?

I wanted to know what they were thinking and feeling and if they wanted to give up and why they didn't. I wanted to know how they moved through the hard stuff to INSPIRED LIVING!

The power of story is a life force. We tell them,

share them, laugh over them, cry in them, find comfort, and heal. We create them, re-write them, shorten them, rephrase them, adapt them but above all we remember them and we treasure them.

They are part of all of us. They are part of the human experience. Stories give life to lessons and blessings. Stories provide us with wisdom and grace, and when shared, we multiply the blessing of story.

ABOUT THE INSPIRED LIVING AND INSPIRED BUSINESS BOOK SERIES

I heard the stories and knew they needed to be shared. This has become my heart project and I will continue to publish new volumes each year.

INSPIRED LIVING
is a collaborative book project all about life.

INSPIRED BUSINESS
is a collaborative book project all about business.

If you enjoy listening to podcasts, I have also interviewed the authors and the series of INSPIRED LIVING podcast interviews can be found on iTunes or Stitcher, under my GET HAPPY NOW Podcast.

If you would like to learn more about the INSPIRED LIVING and INSPIRED BUSINESS book series, please visit: https://jennifersparks.ca/inspired-book-series/

Applications for inclusion in these books can be found at the above website and I encourage you to apply if you have a story that calls to be shared.

~Jennifer Sparks, STOKE Publishing

PLEASE LEAVE A REVIEW

Thank you for spending your time with us!

If you have enjoyed INSPIRED LIVING, we would greatly appreciate it if you would take the time to leave a review on Amazon (paperback or Kindle version) or share INSPIRED LIVING with your friends on social media.

Please tag your shares @stokepub on Facebook and @jennifersparks.inspirethefire on Instagram and use hashtags #inspiredliving #stokepublishing.

Thank you!

www.ingramcontent.com/pod-product-compliance
Lightning Source LLC
Chambersburg PA
CBHW022102090426
42743CB00008B/687